# PRISON PRIVATIZATION: A STUDY OF THE CAUSES AND MAGNITUDE

# PRISON PRIVATIZATION: A STUDY OF THE CAUSES AND MAGNITUDE

## YIJIA JING

Nova Science Publishers, Inc.
*New York*

For permission to use material from this book please contact us:
Telephone 631-231-7269; Fax 631-231-8175
Web Site: http://www.novapublishers.com

LIBRARY OF CONGRESS CATALOGING-IN-PUBLICATION DATA
Jing, Yijia.
Prison privatization : a study of the causes and magnitude / Yijia Jing.
p. cm.
Includes bibliographical references and index.
ISBN 978-1-60692-797-7 (softcover)
1. Prisons--United States. 2. Privatization--United States. I. Title.
HV9469.J56 2009
338.4'7365973--dc22
2008050272

*Published by Nova Science Publishers, Inc.* ✦ *New York*

# DEDICATION

*To my parents*

# CONTENTS

# PREFACE

Dr. Yijia Jing breaks new ground in his sophisticated study of prison privatization in the United States. Jing tackles head-on alternative explanations for the privatization of prisons using American data. He looks at the privatization phenomenon through the prism of the wide variety of practices across the American states. As he notes, the privatization phenomenon is not merely a dichotomous function of yes or no, it also varies in form across the states and those variations may be every bit as important as to whether there is any privatization at all. These variations include, among other things, private ownership of prison facilities, the private contracting of many of the functions of prisons, and the offloading of prisoners to facilities in other states. In sum, privatization is not an "it". Rather, Dr. Jing emphasizes, privatization takes a variety of forms.

Beyond the complexity of the forms privatization can take, Jing's study also identifies what he calls "instrumental" and "political" explanations for privatization. Briefly, instrumental factors refer to those that are economically rational, for example, the higher wages paid to personnel in publicly run institutions than in privately run ones. Labor cost differentials would be expected to provide impetus to the drive toward privatizing prisons. Privatized prisons are less expensive but in part that is because they also have a lower risk share of the prison inmate population. The lower wages in the private sector prisons, however, are to some extent offset by significantly greater turnover and by substantially less pre-service training among their personnel. An alternative explanatory pathway is what Jing identifies as "political". The political explanations have to do with choices made about punitiveness and the consequent higher rate of incarceration in some states more than others owing mainly to ideological differences in methods of crime control. As is often the case, the pathways are not exclusive. Both political explanations and instrumental ones often do well. Measures of state liberalism, for instance, have significant and inverse influences on prison privatization but cost per inmate (an indicator of support system costs) are also significant and positively related to privatization.

Jing's book demonstrates an extraordinarily acute and sensitive understanding of the variety of cultures across the American states and how these interact with instrumental considerations. He goes beyond his large scale data base to control for states with similar instrumental problems but different politics. Here, the choice to privatize or not seems to be based on the politics of the state despite the similar instrumental problems the states face.

Ironically, Jing notes that the instrumental cost issues that push some of the states toward privatizing their prisons in significant ways are often the result of punitive conservative values aimed at retribution rather than rehabilitation. As Jing emphasizes, explaining the privatization phenomenon in prison systems requires taking "political dynamics as a fundamental beginning point, not vice versa." In sum, the dysfunctions of the various state criminal justice systems in the US are the driving force of the privatization boom in prisons.

This is a book that needs to be read to understand (1) how conservative political values have contributed to a warping of the criminal justice system, and (2) the extent to which privatization (which seems to be recently deceased in view of the collapse of the world economic order) is itself driven by a powerful ideological agenda. This outstanding book reflects the value of modern social science in uncovering the mysteries of differential response in the face of often similar pressures.

Bert A. Rockman
Purdue University

# ACKNOWLEDGMENTS

I wish to thank my advisors, Professor Bert Rockman and Professor Trevor Brown, for inspiring my interest in this research and for generously and patiently offering me intellectual support. Their help is indispensable to any success of this research. I thank Professor Anand Desai and Professor Robert Greenbaum for their many insightful critiques and suggestions. I am grateful to Dr. Douglas McDonald and Professor Bayon Price for warmly providing me with their original studies. My gratitude also goes to Professor E.S. Savas for his very insightful suggestions that contributed to the final revisions of the book.

# INTRODUCTION

Since the 1970s, the privatization movement has greatly reshaped the provision of governmental services in western industrialized nations; governments have changed from being direct full service providers to the assemblers and overseers of an array of services formerly deemed public monopolies. In the United States (US), the privatization of government services extends from municipal garbage collection to space programs of the National Aeronautics and Space Administration (Kettl, 1993; Behn and Kant, 1999). Gradually, privatization has penetrated areas that are traditionally thought of as core functions of the state, such as the maintenance of law-and-order, the preparation of congressional testimony, and drafting of policy, especially in Anglo-American countries (Bowman, Hakim, and Seidenstat, 1992; General Accounting Office [GAO],[1] 1991; Kettl, 1993).

Compared to peripheral governmental functions whose privatization may be well explained by economic theories, the privatization of core functions fails to sufficiently justify by economic theories. A further puzzle regarding the privatization of core functions is its violation of the Weberian mandate of state monopoly on core governmental functions. It reverses the century-long efforts of modern state building that pursued the concentration of core functions, especially the legitimate use of physical force, to governments. Markets are utilized in producing services that essentially are not evaluated according to economic efficiency but to political and institutional values. These puzzles ask for a new explanatory logic that makes sense of the privatization of core governmental functions.

---

[1] The General Accounting Office was renamed the Government Accountability Office in July 2004. The abbreviation of GAO remains unchanged.

This research attempts to understand the causes of the privatization of core functions by studying state prison privatization (SPP) in the US. My theoretical framework on the privatization of core functions demonstrates that economic theories may provide incomplete or wrong explanations, while politics are, in general, a driving force of the privatization of core functions. This logic is applied to SPP for empirical verification. Imprisonment is traditionally a core governmental function, and the US is the world leader in prison privatization.[2] The US practice in prison privatization mainly takes the form of SPP, by which state prisoners are imprisoned by private management firms that contract with state governments. SPP in the US provides an excellent opportunity to comparatively examine why governments decide to privatize core functions, partially due to its clear and easy measurement compared to the privatization of other core functions, such as national defense.[3] This research will examine two questions. First, what are the driving forces behind the transfer of the authority to incarcerate prisoners to private for-profit firms in the US? Second, what explains the variation among states in their magnitude of SPP?

# AN EXPLANATION OF STATE PRISON PRIVATIZATION IN THE US

Private management of prisons has blossomed into a vibrant industry since January 1986, when the Marion Adjustment Center in St. Marys, Kentucky became the first private prison in the US to receive state prisoners. From 1986 to 2000, an average of 17 new private prisons entered the marketplace annually. In 2003, 73,675 state prisoners were in private correctional facilities, accounting for 5.7 percent of state prisoners in the US (Bureau of Justice Statistics [BJS], 2004a). The prison privatization boom has spurred heated scholarly debates over its historical roots, causes, and various consequences (Donahue, 1988, 1989; Logan, 1990; Shichor, 1995; Thomas et al., 1997; McDonald et al., 1998, 2003; Camp and Gaes, 2001; Price, 2002; Nicholson-Crotty, 2004). Most recently, the 2004 Iraq Abu Ghraib prison scandal, in

---

[2] In 1996, the rated capacity of private adult secure correctional facilities in the world is 50,628. The US accounted for 92% of it (Thomas, et al., 1997).

[3] State prison systems have state prisoners as direct service recipients and the privatization level can be easily measured by the percentage of prisoners outsourced. For other criminal justice functions, such as policing and sentencing, there are no such data. For national defense, there is no effective way to measure the proportion of war fighting that is outsourced.

which the interrogation of prisoners of war was partially contracted out to private firms, focused public attention on the appropriateness of prison privatization. The case highlights how privatization of core government services raises important accountability questions – both of private contractors and the contracting agency (Mariner, 2004).

SPP refers to the transfer of state prisoners to private correctional facilities operating under contract to state correctional authorities.[4] While contracting out the incarceration of prisoners has been preceded by a variety of service-contracting in state prisons (e.g., prisoner health care, treatment programs, and food services), the delegation of law enforcement authority to private firms raises more fundamental questions about public governance of core government services. It is theoretically and practically important to measure the actual development of SPP and to explain differences among the states. Although SPP is a nationwide movement and 40 states had adopted one or more SPP contracts at some point between 1986 and 2003, there is considerable variation in the magnitude of SPP across the states. States display different levels of "privateness" (Bozeman, 1987) and varying levels of commitment to and dependence on privatized prisons. For example, in 2003, 30 states outsourced prisoners to private facilities, with a range from 0.2% (South Carolina) to 44.2% (New Mexico) in the percentage of state prisoners outsourced, and from 25 (South Dakota) to 16,570 (Texas) in the number of state prisoners outsourced (BJS, 2004a).

Understanding this *variation* is important in that SPP decisions are not only an issue of yes or no, but also, principally, an issue of degree, especially when 40 states had adopted SPP in 2003. While no state has privatized their entire prison population, states that have elected to privatize commit to the practice in varying degrees. In 2003, the SPP levels of the 50 states ranged from 0 to 44.2%, with 20 states having a value of 0 and 20 states having a value below 10%.[5] It is possible that the states that adopted SPP are as or more diverse than they are in relation to those states that never have privatized. In other words, there are two state populations with respect to states that have adopted SPP: those that had limited levels of privatization, even a 0 level in some years, and those that significantly privatized. To date, research has focused on SPP as an "on/off" phenomenon: the adoption of SPP or the existence of an SPP contract. This approach fails to provide a complete picture

---

[4] Adult state prisoners constitute the overwhelming majority of the state prisoner population. In 2000, state prisoners under age 18 accounted for 0.35% of all state prisoners and accounted for 0.18% of state prisoners in private facilities (BJS, 2003).

[5] Ten of the 20 states with a 0 level of SPP in 2003 adopted SPP before 2003.

of SPP (ref. Section 1.5). The level of privatization may reveal as much, if not more, information than the threshold decision to privatize. For example, some SPP states made use of SPP as a short-term substitute and they may be more identified with states that never had an SPP contract. By examining the level of "privateness" of state prison systems, I contribute to the stock of knowledge on SPP in particular, and the privatization of core government functions more generally.

This research approaches the privatization of core government functions from multiple disciplines, with an emphasis on the perspective of politics. As the political landscape surrounding government services evolves, the sentiment about the "publicness" of each service changes. Core government functions accrue their status as central to the state's function and operation because they are politically defined as such. In the case of the core government function of incarceration, prison privatization is first, a result of the rise of conservatism in social control and neoliberalism in economic policies since the 1970s. These political trends have reshaped the environment and tasks, and subsequently the operation, of correctional systems in the US. Conservative social control attributes the cause of crime to individual rational choice rather than adverse social conditions. This philosophy requires a punishment-centered custodial state as a primary form of crime control and resorts to the use of extended criminalization and toughened sentencing and correctional administration. As a result, despite decreasing crime rates, new criminal justice policies directly induce the explosion of prisoner populations, thus the functional dilemmas of correctional systems: unconstitutional overcrowding, increased budgeting pressures, and sky-rocketing per resident burden. While instrumental demands for cheaper and less overcrowded correctional facilities directly challenge the monopoly of public corrections and favor prison privatization, they are fundamentally a byproduct of the politicization of criminal justice policies. Further, functioning of instrumental demands on SPP has to be contingent on states' attitudes toward the cause of crime, which position the political and moral barriers toward prison privatization.

Meanwhile, the rise of neoliberal economic policies promotes a minimal and an indirect state apparatus. Neoliberal ideology makes it an obligation for the state to transfer correction-related government expenditures spending to the private sector. Governments are also encouraged to seek cost efficiency by going to private markets. Prison privatization reconciles the conflict between the expansive role of government in social control under social conservatism and the minimal, non-intrusive role of the state across policy areas under neo-liberalism. Through prison privatization, the state simultaneously enhances its overall punishing capacity but reduces its role in the direct administration of punishment.

To sum, political factors are the fundamental driving forces behind SPP, while instrumental factors directly influence SPP. A political economy perspective is necessary for explaining the rise of SPP. The punitive inclination in crime control creates the high demand function on corrections, and neoliberal economic ideology favors alternative ways of meeting the demand, mainly through markets. The prison crisis, often reflected by instrumental problems such as overcrowding and financial unhealthiness, is rooted in politics and their solutions are highly conditioned by political contexts.

The above analytical logic is not limited to the "on/off" SPP decision; rather, the influences of political and instrumental factors are better revealed by the incremental changes over time, thus the cumulated development in SPP. This research argues that variation in SPP among the states is not merely a function of the presence or absence of instrumental factors, such as overcrowding and fiscal conditions that oblige cost efficiency, but rather that there is an underlying political explanation to consider as well. The political environment of each state influences the importance of instrumental factors in determining whether states privatize a portion of their prison population and at what level. This may help to explain the seemly odd facts that states with relatively overcrowded prison systems and high per inmate operating costs tend to have high level of SPP. In Chapter 5, a comparison between New York and New Mexico shows that while they are similar in instrumental aspects, their stark difference regarding SPP can only be explained by politics.

My empirical research design applies this analytical logic to analyzing the variation of the magnitude of SPP among US states in 2003. Political and instrumental factors identified by the theoretical analysis will be tested. The data are cross-sectional. Due to the time lag between the SPP decisions and the actual transfer of prisoners and due to the growth curve of the private prison industry (ref. Section 4.4), data of explanatory variables are mainly collected from 1995 and 1996. Since the dependent variable, the magnitude of SPP, is censored with 20 states having a value of 0 and the other 30 states ranging from 0.2% and 44.2%, the Tobit model will be used for statistical analysis (ref. Sections 4.4 and 4.5). The Tobit analysis can help to disclose the influences of explanatory variables on the magnitude of SPP states that outsource prisoners, and on the probability of outsourcing prisoners for non SPP states that have no prisoners outsourced.

## CONTRIBUTIONS TO RESEARCH AND PRACTICE

By identifying and disentangling the underlying causes of SPP, this research brings clarity to the SPP policy debate. The analyses conducted here show that the adoption and magnitude of SPP reflect the underlying political tastes of states for social control and neo-liberalism, rather than simply a rational response to pragmatic conditions like over-crowding. In addition, the research lays out issues that are important in evaluating whether SPP achieves its purported policy goals given its inherently political roots.

This research also makes several important contributions to academic scholarship on the privatization of core government services, notably the privatization of state prisons. First of all, this study redresses the imbalance between instrumental and political factors in the privatization literature. The current privatization literature is dominated by economic theories that assume the economic rationality of governments. While politics is frequently mentioned, its role in driving the privatization process is not well explained, substantiated, and empirically examined. My research on the privatization of prisons demonstrates how economics must be embedded in the political contexts to gain explanatory power. By examining the underlying political economy of SPP, this research provides a vantage point to reconcile the roles of politics and economics in privatization.

Also, this study discloses some fundamental characteristics of privatization in the policy arena of criminal justice. Studies on SPP show that imprisonment, as one major component of criminal justice systems, is not only a core function but also has its specific features such as different regional traditions, internal political logic, a noncompetitive market, and the nature of state coercion. These features are common to the criminal justice arena. While the privatization potential in justice areas is growing and has recently attracted more attention,[6] it is important to be aware of these characteristics in both theoretical analysis and practical decision making. The analysis of these factors sets a good foundation for future privatization research in criminal justice areas.

Further, by examining the magnitude of SPP, this research builds on the limited "on/off" nature of previous research. Since 1999, the US Bureau of Justice Statistics (BJS) has published annual data that record the percentage of state prisoners under private custody. Using these data adds important information that is not captured by existing research.

---

[6] In 1999, criminal justice expenditures accounted for 7.7% of local and state direct expenditures.

Finally, this research examines SPP activities up to 2003. This provides two advantages to my research. One is that the analysis undertaken here utilizes the most recently available data and reflects the most recent conditions of SPP in the US. Another is that my research covers both the growth and stagnation of SPP: the growth rate of SPP has slowed from an annual rate of 45 percent from 1995 to 1999 to 2.25 percent from 1999 to 2003 (BJS, 2003). This abrupt change has not yet been fully analyzed by existing academic literature. As a result, this research is able to examine the unexpected decline in the growth of SPP in recent years and can tentatively predict future trends of SPP.

## A ROAD MAP OF THE BOOK

In Chapter 1, I lay out the basic research questions. After reviewing the debate in the privatization literature on the causes of privatization, I analyze the privatization of core governmental functions to set the theoretical rationale for the research. I then provide an overview of SPP (history, definition, patterns, and core concepts), analyze the research questions, and review the literature. In Chapter 2, I analyze the markets, services, and performance of private prisons, with a purpose to examine whether economic incentives can be a fundamental driving force of SPP. In Chapter 3, I demonstrate that prison privatization has been driven by two fundamental transformations in the governing philosophy of the US since the 1970s: the rise of conservatism in social control and the ascendancy of neo-liberalism in restructuring the whole economy and the government. I also employ a path-dependent view on SPP and explore the historical roots of SPP in southern states. In Chapter 4, I discuss the measurement of SPP, make assumptions about the decision rationality of SPP decision-makers, explain the data, and introduce the Tobit statistical model. In Chapter 5, I report the results of the Tobit analysis. The empirical results indicate that both political and instrumental factors influence the magnitude of SPP, with political factors conditioning the influences of instrumental factors. In Chapter 6, I summarize empirical findings, discuss policy implications, and suggest directions for future research.

# Chapter 1

# AN OVERVIEW

## INTRODUCTION

In this chapter I establish the general theoretical framework for the exploration of the causes of state prison privatization (SPP). After a review of current debates on the causes of privatization, I examine the privatization of core governmental functions to identify the effects of instrumental and political factors. Specifically, I review the development of SPP since the 1980s, define SPP and identify its patterns, clarify core concepts and research questions, and review the literature on what led to prison privatization in the US.

## 1.1. BASIC PATTERNS OF PRIVATIZATION

"Privatization means different things and takes different forms" (Handler, 1996, p.78). It is more meaningful and viable to investigate its practical patterns than to find an accurate definition. In general, two fundamental modalities of privatization can be identified. Privatization can work through sale of assets or shedding of functions that are no longer perceived as appropriate for public ownership or operation. Underlying this modality is the new conceptualization and prescription for the proper scope of government. The second modality of privatization, which is used in this research, refers to the substitution of the private sector for government agencies in carrying out governmental responsibilities through contracting out, voucher or other means. The substitutive effect is reflected by public financing, delegation of authority, private delivery of governmental services, and probably new government regulations. These two modalities of privatization have respective concerns on "what to do" and "how to do," although they often coexist in privatization practices.

The second modality of privatization can be further divided into two subtypes. The first subtype is termed "basic privatization," referring to the transfer of existing services to the private sector. The second subtype, "extended privatization," does not directly affect the operation of government agencies. Extended privatization satisfies new demands on governmental services. Under extended privatization, the current workload of government agencies is not reduced. It denies the static view of privatization as a zero-sum game. The resulting privatization level, referring to the proportion of public expenditures spent on hiring private contractors, may increase, decrease, or remain unchanged, depending on the original privatization level and the share of new expenditures between private contractors and government agencies. Both public and private sectors can increase in scale under extended privatization. For example, government can decide not to recruit police officers for a new residential area but to hire a private security firm to satisfy the new demand for public security. Again, in some situations basic privatization and extended privatization coexist in the same process.

By avoiding direct cutback to government organizations, extended privatization is politically and operationally easier than basic privatization.[1] Due to the resistance from existing government organizations, the markets of privatization may be divided and the privatization of some services may be largely restricted to new demands. One example is the privatization of core functions that will be explored in this research. As a matter of fact, the resistance to the privatization of core functions may not necessarily be more effective than that to the privatization of peripheral functions if the difference between basic and extend privatization is considered. In terms of the feasibility of privatization, it matters which kind of services are to be privatized, and sometimes it matters more in which ways these services are privatized.

---

[1] Avoidance of competition between public and private service producers through extended privatization is not absolute. If newly provided services to some extent substitute old services, or when the demand for the same service stops increasing or shrinks, public production agencies will still face the pressures of basic privatization.

## 1.2. DEBATES ON THE CAUSES OF PRIVATIZATION

Since the 1970s, privatization has firmly established its role in the production and delivery of governmental services in the US. Contracting out is the major tool of privatization in the US (Dehoog, 1984; Starr, 1990; Handler, 1996). Due to the enormous discretion of governments in the make-or-buy decision on various governmental services, there is theoretical difficulty in explaining the underlying forces that encourage or inhibit governments' "buy" decisions and in explaining the enormous variation across local governments. Although it is well accepted that there are multiple forces behind privatization (Savas, 1987, 2000; Hodge, 2000), there is little literature that intentionally differentiates the various subtle ways that these forces may work together. Basically, there are two major kinds of explanations: instrumental and political. The instrumental explanation argues that governments privatize for higher operational efficiency and effectiveness; that is, for cost savings, for needed capital and expertise, and for doing better with less (Hanke, 1985; Salamon, 1989; GAO, 1991; Gormley, 1999). Alternatively, the political explanation argues that politicians privatize because of a desire to have a smaller government, preference for a market-based government, eagerness to reward political allies, antipathy to unionization, and regional and global policy transfer (Starr, 1990; Ikenberry, 1990; Pierson, 1994). The controversy between these two perspectives extends the classical dispute between the administrative rationality and the political rationality of government (March and Olsen, 1983) to the area of privatization and constitutes a major source of ambiguity in explaining privatization decisions.

Existing research on privatization decisions reflects a dominance of economic theories. Economic theories tend to treat governments as economically rational organizations that operate in an institution-free environment. The advantage for governments to privatize their services, claimed by these theories, is in general based on the assumption that a competitive market exists. A competitive market will force contractors to reduce costs and respond to consumer preferences, although markets sometimes fail to deliver on the promise of competition (Kettl, 1993; Sclar, 2000). Competition is the driving force behind the potential benefits of market: "The profit-seeking firm is potentially a far superior institution for efficient production," yet "that production potential can be tapped only under certain circumstances. Public versus private matters, yet competitive versus noncompetitive usually matters more" (Donahue, 1989, p.78).

Neo-institutional economic theories further use the properties of services and the transaction-related risks and costs to measure the level of market friction and the appropriateness of using markets to govern the transactions. For example, Transaction Cost Theory argues that transaction-specific investment and service measurability will greatly determine the risk taking between governments and contractors, the level of transaction cost, and thus the economic feasibility of contracting out (Brown and Potoski, 2003). If governments can clearly specify and measure service quantity and quality, anticipate future uncertainty, effectively award and punish contractors, and start and end transactions like in a flea market, then there is a chance for governments to hold market power, harness the incentives of profit-seeking, do more and better with less, and do away with inefficient bureaucracy.

The empirical literature demonstrates strong support for these arguments. For example, by using the International City/County Management Association (ICMA) data, Hefetz (2004) shows that contracting out of municipal services is based on the calculation of cost economizing potential and is contingent on factors of principal-agent problems, government management, monitoring and citizen concerns, and market structure. As a corollary, "contract back-in" is also a natural alternative to external service delivery. Warner and Hebdon (2001) research the tools of local governments in New York State to structure markets and find that privatization is mainly based on pragmatic concerns on information, monitoring, and service quality. Hirsch (1995) researches the contracting out of local solid waste disposal and concludes that "political and ideological factors appear to be less determinative than economic considerations" (p.226).

The dominance of economic theories creates two dilemmas. One is that in practice it leads to the ideologized use of economic arguments for privatization. While economic theories are cautious and contingent in concluding the relative cost-efficiency between in-house production and contracting out, privatization decisions in real life may lack a prudent investigation of market structure and service properties. Privatization may be taken for granted as effective and efficient without valid evidence. As the scope of privatization continues to expand and the level of privatization deepens, unexpected negative results also cumulate.

Another dilemma is that in the theoretical literature, the dominance of economics creates an ironical situation that politics is widely noticed but little explored. "The politics of privatization has not received a great deal of attention in the literature or popular press" (Greene, 2002, p.144). Politics emphasizes symbols, appeals to public opinions (or prejudices), and gains legitimacy and power by manipulating public discourses. Slyke (2003, p.307) argues that "privatization and contracting for social services with nonprofit providers was used for politically symbolic reasons to demonstrate that government is getting smaller, working more efficiently by disengaging itself from direct service delivery, and not encroaching on private market." While political and instrumental factors may both exert influence on privatization decisions, in the current literature the exploration on the underlying causal sources of privatization is overwhelmed by approximate explanations that fail to differentiate the effects of political and economic factors.

By looking at the privatization of core governmental functions, this research intends to restore the balance of instrumental and political factors. For this purpose, I will use SPP as a case of the privatization of core governmental functions and disclose the internal political and instrumental logics. Before analyzing SPP, the next section analyzes the privatization of core governmental functions in order to establish the theoretical framework of discussion for the whole research.

## 1.3. A Discussion on the Privatization of Core Governmental Functions

Core governmental functions are the essence of political governance and most profoundly reflect the relation between the state and its members. The special importance of these functions makes it necessary for the state to recognize them as inherently governmental and "buffer" them from external uncertainty and challenges (Thompson, 1967). Despite the critical importance of core functions, they are "difficult to define" (GAO, 1991, p.4). The scope of governmental functions evolved and expanded over time (Stillman, 1996). The border between core and peripheral functions was historically formed and has changed over time. Since governments in theory and in practice have incentives to grow (Tullock, 1965; Downs, 1967; Niskanen, 1971; Oates; 1985), the relevance to carefully determine core functions is necessary only when empire-building impulses face serious constraints that make it necessary to ascertain the priorities of various governing activities.

There are two major views that theorize core governmental functions. First is the more restrictive Weberian legalistic view. This view emphasizes the sharp legal distinction between the state and the society and requires the monopoly of the making, execution, and implementation of laws by the impersonal state. "A state is a human community that (successfully) claims the monopoly of the legitimate use of physical force within a given territory" (Weber, 1946, p.78). A state differentiates itself from any other political, social and economic organizations by its exclusive use of force in realizing its ends. Non-state actors can only legally use force under the authorization of the state. This view came into being during the early formation and developing stages of modern states and emphasizes the inviolable role of the state to rule. It emphasizes the inherent "stateness" of the use of physical force and highlights the potential risk of harming public authority and accountability when functions related to sovereignty and coercion are administered by non-state actors (Moe, 1987).

Another view is more pragmatic and reflects the recent role change of modern states toward service providers. It proposes that the state should be capable of satisfying public needs. For example, the revised Circular A-76 (Office of Management and Budget, 1999) defines "inherently governmental functions" as functions "intimately related to the public interest as to mandate performance by government employees" (p.2). It stipulates the act of governing and the necessary supporting functions to be reserved for in-house production. Light (1999) defines "core competency" of the government as "a skill required for the successful performance of an organization's mission" (p.170). Compared to the holistic Weberian view, this view is more flexible, analytical, and technical in that it can break down the traditionally recognized core functions. For example, national defense can be anatomized into various parts as commercial, governmental, and inherently governmental. The US Department of Defense defines its core function as war fighting (GAO, 2003), but outsources the production of most weapons and even some military tasks (Singer, 2003). Core functions under this perspective are subject to competition between public and private sectors.

In this research I adopt the Weberian view. Core functions are those whose nationalization in history was crucial to the building of modern states. Core functions should be essential to the formation of the political identity of modern states, crucial to the legitimacy and subsistence of the polities, and often involve the use or the threat of force. They constitute the special identity of the state and are excluded from being held by any other organization. Historically, national defense, criminal justice, foreign relations, taxation, management of treasury, and some others were, in general, recognized by modern states as inherently governmental and were monopolized by governments.[2] "All governments maintain control over concentrated means of violence in the form of arms, troops, guards, and jails" (Tilly, 2003, p26). Loss of control of these functions can directly challenge the authority of governments as the only legal representative institution of sovereignty.[3] Comparatively, peripheral governmental functions are not essential for modern state building. What characterizes these functions is not their stateness but their instrumental values, although these functions can also be highly politicized. Yet, the difference between core and peripheral functions is far from self-evident. These functions are, in most situations, institutionally and technically intertwined. Such blurring deepened in that modern state building processes invariably involved the expansion of national administrative capacities (Skowronek, 1982), the scope of which greatly exceeded the core functions. While municipal services like road maintenance and garbage collection can be indisputably identified as peripheral functions, social programs like social security may not be easily defined. Precisely what is a core function is still a much debated matter.

The following section continues this discussion by identifying two basic characteristics of core governmental functions that determine the prospects of their privatization: (1) difficulty in utilizing market mechanisms to improve performance and (2) the political stakes linked to the monopoly of these functions by the state.

## 1.3.1. Two Privatization-related Properties of Core Functions

The privatization of core functions replaces public production units by private firms. Economic logic is utilized in fulfilling core governmental tasks, making it a critical question whether market and core governmental functions can mutually adapt through privatization. Both economic and political properties of core functions may set barriers to privatization.

Economically, core functions are the most difficult in harnessing market mechanisms to enhance performance. Core functions, according to the

---

[2] The US federal government demonstrated a good example of a minimum state with only core functions at its beginning stage. It had only five branches: the State Department, the War Department, the Treasury Department, the Attorney General's Office, and the Postal Services Department (Stillman, 1996).

[3] There are always some exceptions. For example, some modern states practice the hiring of mercenaries in war times. Involvement of private for-profit firms in military operations is growing (Singer, 2003).

economic criteria of nonrivalry and nonexclusiveness, are often classified as pure public goods, which are most likely to be undersupplied or be supplied in less satisfactory quality if left to private markets. Market failures make it necessary for the state to assume responsibility for providing these functions. Yet, market failures do not necessarily entail government monopoly. Governments can limit their responsibility to raising and distributing revenues for these functions and specifying the amount and properties of the services, while letting private firms to do the actual work. The financing (public) and performance (private) can still be separated by contracting out if nongovernment actors can outperform government agencies in service production (Hanke, 1985; Donahue, 1989). Here the critical question is whether governments can effectively coopt private firms and manage the public-private partnership through contracts.

According to Transaction Cost Economics (TCE), the contractibility of core functions is limited for two reasons. One is that the measurability of service efficiency, quality, and effectiveness is very low compared to that of peripheral functions. For example, who can set a quota on the military expenditures in Iraq as a criterion to measure the military efficiency of the Pentagon? Military expenditures are subject to many uncertain factors, including the concern for the safety of US soldiers. Life is not easily quantified by money. Yet, it is relatively convenient for local governments to specify how frequently garbage should be collected and set a price. As public goods, core functions have strong externalities and are inherently difficult for governments to establish objective standards of performance. Meanwhile, the operation of core functions is embedded in a highly institutionalized environment and is under the constraint of various institutions, regulations, check-and-balances, and political competition. Governments may decouple formal organizational structure and actual operation and avoid external inspection and evaluation (Meyer and Rowan, 1977). Under both technical and political uncertainty, performance evaluation is, to a large extent, a political issue. This makes contracts unavoidably incomplete. As an imperfect solution, reliance on procedural control or makeshift instrumental criteria may lead to unintended consequences of goal displacement, which is the very bureaucratic disease (Crozier, 1964) that contracting out intends to cure. Private firms can purposefully take advantage of the "production paradox" (Gregory, 1995), the information asymmetry of which creates opportunities of "self-seeking with guile" (Williamson, 1975).

Another danger that TCE may predict lies in the imperfect market. Core functions are often highly specialized in their uses. These highly specified physical and human investments lead to mutual dependence between the principal and agent, which substitutes market competition with long-term cooperation. Vast political, economic, or legal investments on coordination are induced. Consequently, private contractors will not only be involved in the production process, but also in the institutional process that sets the rules of the game. Sunk costs, as well as institutional embeddedness, make it less likely to shift contractors, thus vitiate the effectiveness of market disciplines. First-mover advantages can be permanent and create long-term entrenchment. As a result, TCE may suggest that governments refrain from privatizing core functions due to their low contractibility.

Politically, core functions are directly related to the fundamental political order and the interests of the state and its organizations. The building process of modern states is based on the formation of two modern governance institutions: the mass-based, competitive, and party-based representative system and the "neutral" administrative system, the bureaucracy (Weber, 1946). State-building is reflected by the universal application of laws made by the representative system and implemented, monopolistically, by the administrative branch. Core functions are the major targets to be modernized and reserved by these modern state infrastructures. Together, these contents and instruments of modern states cultivated broad-based social support for the regime and constituted the basic justifications for the existence of the government. Consequently, core functions are highly ideologized and protected by legal and political principles. The socially constructed "stateness" of these functions became their inherent property over time. Clearly, the appropriateness and necessity of the government to implement these services is not established on a comparative-efficiency rationale, but on the political definition of these functions.

Although the highly normative justifications for public monopoly of core functions tend to be accepted universally as a result of the globalization of modern institutions, the roots of the conception of core governmental functions in different nation states have to be found in their specific historical processes of state building and evolution. States build their specific political identities based on their specific processes of state formation. This makes an exploration from a path-dependent perspective important since different countries may have different historical paths of state building. For example, the state-centered model of Germany made it a mandate of the state to have a far broader scope of public services than the US state that in history had a relatively indirect role in social and economic affairs. Yet invariably, the privatization of core functions in a nation state always imposes a threat to the political values that they represent. Due to political controversy and organizational resistance, core governmental functions are unlikely to be outsourced and are the last to be placed on the privatization agenda.

Assuming the correctness of above analysis, an explanatory logic for the privatization of core functions has to address changes in both political and instrumental areas that overcome the revealed weakness of core functions regarding their contractibility. My analysis has clearly shown that economic properties of core functions are essentially determined by their political attributes. Without the political sphere first changing, there may lack a driving force that would adapt core functions to markets and justify their privatization. As such, I tentatively propose a political economy logic for the privatization of core functions: the causal chain of the privatization of core functions should be fundamentally traced to the changes in political values, while both political and instrumental factors may directly influence the privatization decision of core functions.

## 1.3.2. Imprisonment as a Core Function

One essential element in modern state building was the monopolization of coercive forces by the state. States monopolized the power of war making by establishing centralized military regimes. Civilian disarmament was achieved by establishing public justice systems (Tilly, 1985, 1992). Modern police, courts, and prison systems gradually crowded out the private use of force, and most modern states nationalized fully or largely their punishment systems.

In this research, imprisonment means the implementation stage of the imprisonment decision, which is given by the courts. The analysis has a focus on the prison system. Imprisonment became a core governmental function during the modernization of criminal justice system. "In order that any punishment should not be an act of violence committed by one person or many against a private citizen, it is essential that it should be public, prompt, necessary, and the minimum possible under the given circumstances, proportionate to the crimes, and established by law" (Beccaria, 1986, p.81). In the US, the private imprisonment of state prisoners was ended in the middle of the 20<sup>th</sup> century when full responsibility for their incarceration was taken over by public authorities. The recent return to private corrections in the US and a few other Anglo countries in the 1980s led to challenges to the multicenturylong state-building process and the established political structure and institutions.[4]

Imprisonment is coercive and involuntary. Such power to coerce is fundamental to the state. Compared to imprisonment itself, there are also prison services that maintain the prisoners. These include, among other things, medical services, mental health services, treatment programs, food services, laundry, mail and telephone, religious services, library services, recreation, counseling programs, and education. Many of these services are contracted out to private vendors. Within the correctional system, however, it is imprisonment that constitutes the core while prison services constitute the peripheral. The difference may be similar to that between an army's soldiers and their uniforms.

In reality, the privatization movement penetrates both areas—core and peripheral—but their development is dissimilar.[5] The privatization of both principally involves contracting out, though ultimately, governments are still financially responsible for the correctional costs. Figure 1.1 compares the privatization of imprisonment in 2003 (the percentage of state prisoners under the custody of private contractors) and service-contracting in 1995 (the percentage of prison services outsourced to private contractors) for 41 states. It shows that some states may treat service-contracting and SPP to be qualitatively different, while others do not. All the 41 states except Colorado privatized prison services in 1995, while in 2003 only 24 of them used SPP. For these 24 states, all of them used in-house production for the bulk of public prison services in 1995, and in fact, also in 2003. While Illinois and New York were the only two states that legislatively banned prison privatization, they nonetheless contracted out 8 percent and 2 percent of prison services respectively. A pattern is clear that service-contracting is largely an issue of degree, yet for SPP there can be a yes-or-no choice. Currently, the academic literature on SPP also only researches the yes-or-no side of SPP.

While political and economic theories have the potential to explain the difference among states in SPP, I will leave the task of exploring their explanatory power to subsequent chapters. In the following sections, I review the development of SPP, its definition and patterns, core concepts and research

---

[4] In 2002, Australia, the United Kingdom, South Africa, Canada, and New Zealand also had private correctional facilities (Nathan, 2002).
[5] The privatization of imprisonment entails the transfer of the provision of all prison services to private contractors. These services in private prisons can be either directly produced by the contractors or be further contracted out by them.

questions, and the existing literature, in order to prepare a background for the analysis of SPP in Chapters 2 and 3.

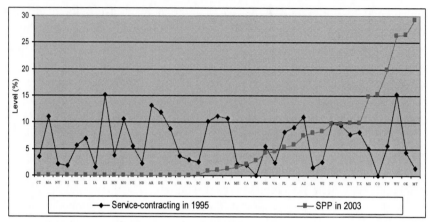

Source: National Institute of Corrections (1996) and Bureau of Justice Statistics (BJS, 2004a).
Note: Service-contracting is based on the share of expenditures. SPP is based on the percentage of prisoners outsourced to private facilities.

Figure 1.1.Services-contracting in 1995 and SPP in 2003, 41 states.

# 1.4. A HISTORICAL REVIEW OF STATE PRISON PRIVATIZATION

Making profit through punishment is nothing new in the US. Compatible with the pervasive penetration by the private sector in criminal justice practice in the 19th century, private imprisonment was a common practice. Private prisons emerged for many reasons including the gradual abolishment of corporal punishment, the insufficient capacity of public prisons, and the commercial interest of the private sector to use convict labor. Since 1825, convict leasing emerged, which put prisoners under full control of private for-profit leasers (Shichor, 1995). "Virtually every state relied on convict labor at some point" (Knepper, 1991, p.16). The retreat of commercial interests from incarceration was driven by the industrialization and modernization of the US society and by the growing tendency of the state to forbid the private use of coercive force. The newly established market order felt the distortion by prison labor, and the notorious prisoner rights abuse records of private prisons also vastly contradicted the growingly accepted rehabilitative ideal of corrections. The US government gradually took imprisonment as a public function immune to profit motives. The convict lease system was repealed in 1923 and the private contract system of prison labor finally disappeared in 1940 when prison labor lost its commercial potential.[6] A full-fledged public prison system came into being. Nonetheless, private operation of correctional facilities continued to exist, especially for community-based and juvenile corrections (Logan, 1990). Besides, public prisons never fully relied on themselves to provide all prison services.

Resurgence of private correctional facilities in the 1980s was not a return to the commercial use of convict labor; rather, it focused on the government's payment for outsourced prisoners. This new round of prison privatization concentrated on the establishment of private adult secure correctional facilities.[7] All contractors operating secure correctional facilities were private for-profit firms. Different levels of governments entered this market at roughly the same time. At the federal level, it was initiated in April 1984 with the opening of Houston Processing Center operated by Corrections Corporation of America (CCA), holding adult illegal aliens for Immigration and Naturalization Service (INS) and convicted alien offenders for Bureau of Prisons (BOP) (Logan, 1990). At the state level, Kentucky initiated SPP by contracting with US Corrections Corporation in 1986 (BJS, 1996). At the local level, Hamilton County, TN first contracted with CCA to imprison its detainees in Texas in 1984. All those initiating private correctional facilities had a minimum security level. In fact, among the 140 private state prisons established between 1995 and 2000, most were minimum or low in security, or community-based.[8] Only one maximum security private facility was built during this period, adding up to a national total of four. In 2000, the per-prison number of inmates for public state prisons was 884, compared to 302 for all private prisons. The private prison industry mainly assumed a complementary role to public prison systems.

---

[6] The *1940 Sumners-Ashurst Act* made it a federal crime to knowingly transport convict-made goods in interstate commerce for private use, regardless of what state law allowed.

[7] Secure facilities refer to confinement institutions in which less than 50% of the residents are regularly permitted to leave, unaccompanied by staff, for work, study, or rehabilitation. Community-based facilities are those in which 50% or more of the residents are regularly permitted to leave.

[8] Private correctional facilities may admit inmates from a sole source or multiple sources. Private prisons admit prisoners from federal or/and state correctional authorities as the majority of the inmates. When they admit state prisoners, they are called private state prisons. In the

In the 1990s, there was a boom of the private prison industry. Figure 1.2 (a-b) shows that of the 204 prisons added between 1995 and 2000 for BOP and state prisoners, three quarters (154) were private (BJS, 2003a). During the same period, federal prisoners held in private facilities increased from 1,018 to 14,841 while state prisoners from 15,408 to 76,343 (BJS, 2003a). In 2002, 12.4% of BOP prisoners and 5.8% of state prisoners were in privately operated correctional facilities.[9] The private sector has been involved in prison financing, construction, and operation. In 1995, the market value of outsourced prison services in 44 states, as reported by the National Institute of Corrections, reached $1.12 billion (National Institute of Corrections, 1996). Meanwhile, the market for full correctional privatization (including private local jails) also burgeoned and reached $1 billion in mid-1997 (Singal and Reed, 1997). Currently, privatization of an entire state prison system has not happened, despite the two failed attempts by CCA to take over the prison system of Tennessee for a 99-year lease agreement (Bates, 1998). The only state prison system that collapsed in recent years, the DC Lorton Correctional Complex, was taken over by Bureau of Prisons (BOP) rather than a private firm in 1997.

The selection of state-level prison privatization as my research focus is due to the importance of state prison systems in the US correctional system. Figure 1.3 (a-b-c) shows that in 2000 state prisoners account for about 60 percent of all inmates and 78 percent of prisoners outsourced. In the same year, private facilities held 5.8 percent of all state prisoners, slightly more than state prisoners imprisoned in local jails, federal facilities, and other state facilities.

---

literature "private prison" may broadly cover all private facilities including those admitting local inmates.

[9] From 1999 to 2001, federal prisoners outsourced to private facilities increased from 3,828 (2.8%) to 19,251 (12.3%). This abrupt change was primarily because of the transfer of DC prisoners to BOP, which started in 1997 and finished on Dec. 31, 2001. In 1996, DC planned to privatize 75% of all its correctional operations by the year 2000 (Florida Corrections Commission, 1996). In 1998, 19% of DC prisoners were in the Northeast Ohio Correctional Center at Youngstown, Ohio, operated by CCA.

Growth of Private Prisons 86-00

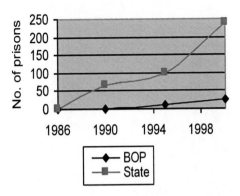

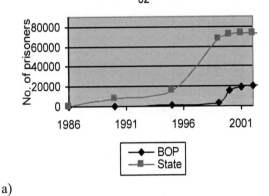

a)                                                                    b)

Source: BJS (2000a, 2001, 2002a, 2003a-b, 2004a)

Figure 1.2. Growth of prison privatization in the US.

Figure 1.4 shows the cumulative percentage of states that practiced SPP between 1986 and 2003. The late 1990s was a major period of the entry of states into SPP. Figure 1.2 also shows that the scale of SPP expanded quickly in the same period and then grew slowly. While in 2003 only 30 states outsourced prisoners, Figure 1.4 shows that 80% of states (40 states) had adopted SPP up to 2003. This indicates that compared to the adoption of SPP, the actual prisoner outsourcing is a flexible and reversible process. States that adopted SPP may maintain one or more or no SPP contracts at different points of time. The importance of this phenomenon will be further discussed in Section 1.6 and in Section 4.1.

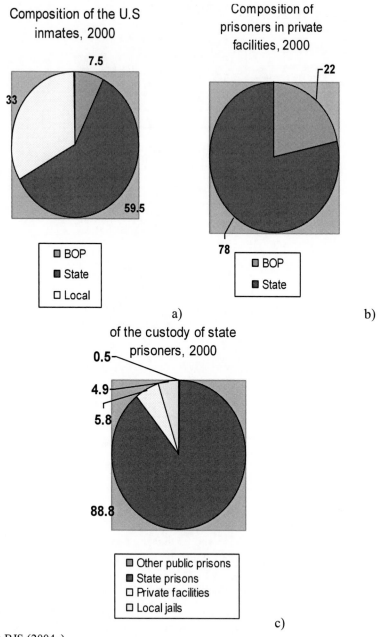

Composition of the U.S inmates, 2000

7.5

33

59.5

☐ BOP
■ State
☐ Local

a)

Composition of prisoners in private facilities, 2000

22

78

☐ BOP
■ State

b)

of the custody of state prisoners, 2000

0.5

4.9

5.8

88.8

☐ Other public prisons
■ State prisons
☐ Private facilities
☐ Local jails

c)

Source: BJS (2004c).

Figure 1.3. Composition of the US correctional inmates, prisoners in private facilities, and state prisoners, 2000.

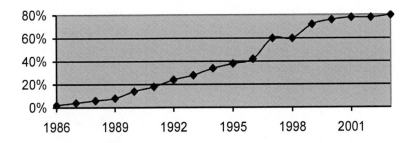

Figure 1.4. Percentage of states that had outsourced prisoners, 1986-2003.

## 1.5. DEFINITION AND PATTERNS OF STATE PRISON PRIVATIZATION

SPP is defined as the transfer of state prisoners to private facilities under contract to state correctional authorities. It belongs to the second modality of privatization by which governments maintain responsibility for the financing of corrections, while leaving their operation to contractors. Outsourced prisoners are still under the legal authority of state governments but are under the direct custody of private firms. Private correctional facilities are those that are operated by private firms. Private state prisons receive the majority of outsourced state prisoners.[10] Local private facilities may also contract with state governments.[11] This definition of SPP is very restrictive in that it entails the delegation of incarceration authority from state governments to private firms through contracts. Outsourcing of specific prison services to private firms, such as medical services, and the usage of market financial instruments, such as the construction-lease arrangement, do not involve the transfer of

---

[10] According to *Census of State and Federal Correctional Facilities, 2000* (BJS, 2003), private state prisons are adult correctional facilities operating under contract to state correctional authorities, including places of confinement such as prisons, prison hospitals, prison farms, boot camps, and centers for reception, classification, or alcohol and drug treatment; and community-based facilities such as halfway houses, group homes, and work release centers.

[11] According to Bureau of Justice Statistics, prisons are facilities with 50% or more of their inmates held for State or Federal correctional authorities, while facilities with more than 50% of their inmates held for local authorities are classified as jails. Sole-source contracts with state governments lead to private state prisons, while spec-facility may be defined as local facility since it may accept inmates from various levels of governments and from various regions. Private local facilities admit a small portion of the outsourced state prisoners.

custody and are defined as partial prison privatization. In contrast, SPP is full prison privatization.[12] Transfer of prisoners through SPP requires that private contractors provide the full range of prison services, which can be further outsourced by the contractors.

Table 1.1 shows four patterns of the 50 states' involvement in SPP, according to the jurisdiction of outsourced prisoners and the location of private facilities. Pattern I indicates that states contract out prisoners to in-state facilities. This is the most common SPP practice. Pattern II indicates that states export prisoners to facilities in other states. Only in these two situations are states involved in SPP by making the outsourcing decision. Pattern III indicates that prisoners from other states are imported by in-state private facilities. The states in which the facilities are located do not have legal jurisdiction over these prisoners and thus are not really involved in SPP. For pattern IV, states neither contract out prisoners nor accommodate private facilities. Table 1.1 also shows that in 2000, 12 states had nothing to do with SPP, for example Rhode Island and Vermont; 7 states did not contract out prisoners but made money by importing prisoners from other states, for example Illinois and Minnesota; 4 states only outsourced prisoners to out-of-state facilities, for example Michigan and Wisconsin; 27 states outsourced prisoners to in-state facilities. These 27 states may also export or import prisoners at the same time. A total of 31 states were involved in SPP in 2000.

**Table 1.1. Patterns of states' involvement in SPP, 2000**

|  |  | **Jurisdiction of outsourced state prisoners** | |
|  |  | Yes | No |
| **Facility location** | In state | In-state SPP (I) 27 | Prisoner import (III) 7 |
|  | Out of state | Prisoner export (II) 4 | (IV) 12 |

Source: BJS (2001) and BJS (2003a). The former source provides the jurisdiction count of prisoners in private prisons, and the latter provides the custody count.

Note: The Arabic number indicates the number of states falling into the corresponding types in 2000

---

[12] Leonard (1990) differentiates nominal and operational prison privatization, with the former referring to "transferring the ownership of the prison facility to private hands" and the latter referring to the "substitution of private for public operation of correctional facilities." Prison privatization in this research corresponds to the second type.

**Table 1.2. Four types of prison privatization arrangements**

|  |  | Facility Ownership | |
|---|---|---|---|
|  |  | Public | Private |
| **Facility Construction** | Old | Management replacement (Type 3) | Sale of asset (Type 4) |
|  | New | Introduce private management to public facilities (Type 2) | Outsource prisoners to private facilities (Type 1) |

Note: Outsourcing of prisoners is assumed for every arrangement.

Table 1.2 shows four types of SPP arrangements according to facility construction and ownership. The common element in these four types is the private management of facilities. The most common type of SPP is type 1, showing the feature of SPP as "extended privatization" driven by increasing demand. According to McDonald, et al. (1998), in 1997, 50 (60%) of the 84 facilities that contract with state or federal correctional agencies were owned by private firms. In 2004, 38 (60%) of the 63 facilities of Corrections Corporation of America (CCA) were owned by CCA.[13] From type (1) to type (4),[14] there is a sequentially decline in feasibility. McDonald et al. (2003) differentiate private prison markets as the dominant sole-source prison market and the complementary spec prison market. Most private prisons were built after being awarded a contract from state governments, while some private firms may risk building facilities before having a contract and then advertise nationwide. The latter facilities are called spec prisons. They admit prisoners from multiple sources, without being limited to states where they are located. In 1997, 15 (18%) of the 84 facilities that contracted with state or federal correctional agencies were spec prisons (McDonald, et al., 1998).

---

[13] See CCA web: http://www.correctionscorp.com/locationsmap.html
[14] Type (4) is the rarest as the divesture of assets. In 1997, DC sold an existing 888-bed correctional treatment facility to CCA for $59 million. CCA would operate it for DC under a 20-year lease-purchase agreement and a 20-year management agreement.

# 1.6. CORE CONCEPTS AND RESEARCH QUESTIONS IN THE SPP DECISION

The unit of analysis for SPP, according to its definition, should be the state that has the legal authority to decide the way of imprisonment. Conceptually, the state can make two consecutive decisions regarding SPP: the yes-or-no decision and the how-much decision, with the first one deciding the value acceptability of SPP, and with the latter one deciding the extent of SPP. Two key concepts, compatible with these qualitative and quantitative aspects of the SPP decision, are the adoption of SPP and the magnitude of SPP.

*Adoption of SPP.* The adoption of SPP is a political concept, indicating the value acceptability of SPP for a state. Nicholson-Crotty (2004) uses the existence of enabling SPP legislation as an indicator of states' political acceptance of SPP. Since a couple of states established SPP contracts without first having pro-SPP legislation, this indicator may not be accurate enough. I will operationalize this concept by looking at the first SPP contract established by states. States adopt SPP when they for the first time have an SPP contract. Thus, the adoption of SPP for every state can only happen once and it is a yes-or-no choice for a state. It is important to notice that states may not outsource prisoners soon after a contract is established. For sole-source contracts, states may have to wait for a couple of years before private facilities are ready to accept prisoners.

*Magnitude of SPP.* The magnitude of SPP, or the level of SPP, reflects the actual reliance of states on private firms to imprison prisoners at certain post-adoption point of time. There are two indicators to measure the magnitude. One is to measure the number of active SPP contracts, starting from 0 to n. Another is to use the percentage of state prisoners incarcerated in private facilities, starting from 0 to 1. There is much coincidence between them, for example, they often have 0 or positive values simultaneously.[15] Since I intend to compare states regarding their reliance on SPP, the percentage indicator is more appropriate. For one thing, it directly discloses the degree of such reliance which the absolute number of SPP contracts may not reflect; for another, only the percentage indicator can accurately reflect the existence of prisoner outsourcing, while the existence of SPP contracts may not necessarily reflect any actual reliance of states on private facilities, due to the temporal lag

---

[15] Both indicators can be further transformed to be a dichotomous variable, with 1 meaning the existence of at least one SPP contract or at least one outsourced prisoner, else 0. Nicholson-Crotty (2004) measures the existence of contracts in the latter way in his research.

between contract making and prisoner outsourcing. In this research, the magnitude of SPP refers to the percentage of state prisoners outsourced to private contractors in a certain year. Overall, the magnitude of SPP has a more flexible decision process and can be adjusted over time for states that have adopted SPP.

Consequently, some relevant concepts are defined:

| | |
|---|---|
| *SPP state*: | A state with at least one prisoner outsourced in a certain year. |
| *Non-SPP state*: | A state with no prisoners outsourced in a certain year. |
| *Swing state*: | A non-SPP state that was once an SPP state. Figure 1.4 shows that in 2003, 40 states were once SPP states, yet only 30 states outsourced prisoners in that year. The 10 swing states in 2003 are Kansas, Minnesota, Missouri, North Dakota, Arkansas, Delaware, Nevada, Oregon, Washington, and Utah. For example, North Dakota began outsourcing prisoners in 1997, ceased in 1999, resumed outsourcing during 2000 and 2002, and then exit again in 2003. |
| *Non-adoption state*: | A state that has never had an SPP contract. In 2003, there were 10 states that have never practiced SPP: Connecticut, Massachusetts, New Hampshire, New York, Rhode Island, Vermont, Illinois, Iowa, Nebraska, and West Virginia. |

According to the two-stage view of SPP decision and the two forms of SPP outputs, there are two possible research questions about SPP. One is to research the causality of SPP, namely why SPP was adopted by some states as a valid policy instrument, with a focus on the adoption of SPP. Another is to research the magnitude of SPP and examine why states have different levels of SPP. In this paper, I will use a historical perspective to explain the rise of SPP as a nationwide phenomenon, and use an empirical analysis to compare the 50 states regarding their magnitude of SPP.

Why I emphasize the variation in the magnitude of SPP rather than the adoption of SPP in the empirical analysis is due to the different richness of these two kinds of information. As has been mentioned in the introduction, the differences in the adoption of SPP may not reflect more information than the differences in the magnitude of SPP. A state that adopted SPP but has a low level of SPP, even 0, may be more similar to a state that has not adopted SPP, than to a state with a very high SPP level. The relevance of this argument is based on the fact that states, after adopting SPP, may be reluctant to deepen their utilization of SPP, or even stop outsourcing prisoners, which the existing empirical literature fails to notice. States that adopted SPP previously may nonetheless have a zero value for their present magnitude of SPP and thus be classified as non-SPP states. Non-SPP, or the nonexistence of prisoner outsourcing, does not necessarily mean non-adoption. As a result, the importance of the adoption of SPP, or the establishing of the first SPP contract, is reduced. It may not set a stable path for states. Focusing on the adoption may ignore post-adoption SPP practices that can be very different. It is also problematic to rely on the existence of SPP contracts, since the existence of SPP contracts may not necessarily mean a simultaneous existence of prisoner outsourcing, and it is also incapable of reflecting the level of states' reliance on SPP.

The above facts make the magnitude of SPP a more interesting empirical phenomenon. Differences in the level of SPP, especially between states with a significant level of SPP and other states, can better explain the stable differences among states and reflect an institutionalization of the privatization route, while simply looking at the existence of SPP contracts or the adoption of SPP may either exaggerate the difference between certain groups of states or waste important information. To explain the variation among states in their magnitude of SPP will be the task of the empirical research of this research, and understanding the causes behind the transfer of imprisonment duties to private firms is a necessary condition for the empirical design. I will discuss the internal causality of SPP in Chapters 2 and 3, and empirically examine the influences of different factors in Chapters 4 and 5.

The general prison privatization literature invariably emphasizes the entry choice, namely the adoption of SPP, but ignores the magnitude of SPP. In the empirical literature, neither the adoption nor the magnitude is clearly defined, measured, and empirically examined. The following section will review the relevant literature.

# 1.7. A Review of the Causes of Prison Privatization in the US

Current academic exploration of prison privatization has different foci. It investigates the historical evolvement and the status quo of the private prison industry in the US (Durham III, 1993; Shichor, 1995; Logan, 1990; McDonald et al., 1998). Unavoidably, it provides analysis of the causal factors and the established patterns of prison privatization (Logan, 1990; McDonald et al., 1998; Price, 2002; Nicholson-Crotty, 2004). Also, performance of private prisons, especially their cost efficiency, is evaluated (Donahue, 1988; McDonald et al., 1998, 2002; GAO, 1996). Finally, economic, social, legal and political consequences of prison privatization are discussed (Shichor, 1995; Logan, 1990; McDonald, 1990; Hart et al., 1997; Donahue, 1988, 1989).

## 1.7.1. Theory-based and Case-based Explanations of State Prison Privatization

This literature review identifies three major kinds of causes of prison privatization: political, pragmatic, and economic. While they are all partially correct, it is critical to place them in the right location of the causal chain of prison privatization, and compare their relative importance. The following chapters will attempt to settle this problem by restructuring and organizing these explanations.

### Political Causes

The literature on prison privatization captures the new trends in the political environment that challenge the necessity and efficiency of public monopoly on imprisonment. The response of various stakeholders is also noticed. Political factors, however, are often hard to operationalize and empirically test.

The rise of neoliberal economic philosophy and practice proposes privatization as a basic way to both reduce the government and reshape its operation. Public-private partnership "utilizes government for what it does best-raising resources and setting societal priorities through a democratic political process-while utilizing the private sector for what it does best-organizing the production of goods and services" (Salamon, 1989, p.10). Under neoliberalism's antipathy to bureaucracy and its favor of commercial interests, private participation in corrections, especially in providing prison services, is deemed as legitimate, necessary and healthy. In 2000, according to the American Federation of State, County, and Municipal Employees, only Illinois and New York had state legislation prohibiting prison privatization; 30 states had legislation authorizing SPP; and the remaining 18 states had permissive interpretation of general statutes. As a result, a state's legal environment in general does not constitute a barrier to SPP.

Tough crime control policies increase the demand for prison capacity. The US criminal justice system experienced a fundamental transformation during the last quarter of the $20^{th}$ century. Crime control policies gradually grew to favor the justice model and shifted the major policy goal from rehabilitation to retribution (Mackenize, 2001). This change increased the demand for private prisons and reduced political and moral entry barriers to prison privatization.

A private prison advocacy coalition imposes political pressure on governments for more prison privatization. Private businesses, not just private prisons, benefit from government contracts and subcontracts. While the private prison industry grew quickly, had its industrial giants, and contributed to the local tax base and employment, risk of state capture by business interests could also increase. For some local governments, building and operating private correctional facilities is a major source of employment opportunities and public revenues (McDonald et al., 2003). Furthermore, prison privatization may be a way to reward political allies. The private prison industry made heavy lobbying efforts in its history and also compensate those producing favorable academic research (Nelson, 2003).

The pursuit of political responsiveness may push the governments into prison privatization. The public correctional system is organized according to various principles of public administration with an emphasis on legal accountability. Multiple principals, agents, and goals, various procedural constraints and regulations, and interorganizational conflicts of interests elongate the chain of command and control and dilute the capacity of the central policy unit in carrying out its policy goals. Contracting out offers the opportunity to evade the complex and frustrating bureaucratic administrative systems and rules by working directly with private producers whose welfare is contingent on their fulfillment of performance criteria specified in contracts. McDonald (1990) observes that local governments may use contracting out to bypass the control of elected sheriffs on jails.

Similarly, governments may privatize prisons for policy autonomy and flexibility that are constrained by public unions. Privatization can work as a way to reduce the power of trade unions (Hodge, 2000). While low level managers and prison workers overwhelmingly oppose prison privatization due to its downward influences on their job security and compensation, high and middle-level correctional officials may want to use privatization to empower themselves and gain more managerial discretion.

## Pragmatic Causes

SPP has the pragmatic goal to improve the capacity in incarcerating state prisoners.

The direct and most urgent cause commonly identified is the pervasive overcrowding of public prison systems. This overcrowding reduces the effectiveness of incapacitation, retribution, and rehabilitation and paralyzes the whole justice system. From 1974 to 2000, the number of state prisons increased from 592 to 1,320 (123% increase), while state prisoners increased from 218,000 to 1,101,202 (405% increase). State governments responded by building large prisons and increasing the capacity of existing prisons to handle the growing demand. In 2000, the average number of inmates in custody for state prisons less than 20 years old, including private prisons,[16] was 851 per prison, almost 200 more than older (665) state prisons (BJS, 2003A). Despite the fast increase of prisons, a serious gap between the demand and supply of prison cells came into being. The mid-1990s saw the worst situation. In 1995, there was a gap of 79,881 between state prisoner population and the rated capacity of state prison systems nationwide.[17] Nineteen percent of this gap was covered by private prisons, while 41% was covered by local jails. In 2000, this gap increased to 143,524. Fifty percent was covered by private prisons, and 42% by local jails. The difficulty of state prisons in housing new prisoners set constraints on the operation of other correctional institutions, the courts and the police. Since 1999 prison overcrowding forced state prisons to retain more than 5.2% of sentenced state prisoners in local jails that were themselves overcrowded. In 2002, only 12 states did not house prisoners in local jails (BJS, 2004a). Some states were sued by counties for their failure to meet their statutory obligation to receive state-convicted felons into prison systems and were fined.[18] The courts and the police, as the "producers" of prisoners, have

---

[16] Of the 264 private prisons, 23 of them contracted with BOP, 238 of them with the states.

[17] Rated capacity is the number of beds or inmates assigned by a rating official to institutions within the jurisdiction.

[18] For example, the *County Nueces, Texas v. Texas Board of Corrections* led to the state's loss and its liability to pay the counties $20 per day for each convicted felon housed in local jails. From Sep 28, 1987 to Feb 28, 1990, Texas owed $100.3 million to its 12 counties (Kerle, 1999).

to reduce the strictness of law enforcement within their discretion to avoid pressuring their correctional colleagues. The court system faces paradoxical situations. While the state courts churned out sentenced prisoners, federal courts often ordered states to limit prison overcrowding, fined them for unconstitutional conditions, and issued orders to reduce the prisoner load.

Lack of, or unwillingness to commit, adequate financial resources at the state level to cope with the increased load, is another reason. Since the 1970s, the correctional system has produced a disproportionate burden on public budgets. Using 1996 constant dollars, annual expenditures on state corrections experienced a 225% increase between 1984 and 1996 from $6.78 billion to $22.03 billion. Simultaneous to this expansion in total expenditures was an increase in the per capita burden from $53 in 1985 to $103 in 1996 (BJS, 1999). Besides, such an increase of expenditure was increasingly absorbed by operating expenditures spent on staff compensation rather than prison capacity expansion. During 1984-1996, the proportion of capital expenditure declined from 13% to 6 % (BJS, 1999). Voters responded by imposing budgetary disciplines. The passage of Proposition 13 in California in 1978, due to the taxpayer rebellion, created a national spread of tax and spending limits legislation (TSL). Until 2004, 27 states had introduced some kind of tax and spending limits legislation (National Conference of State Legislatures, 2004). Because of voters' preferences for both improved crime control and limited capital expenditure in corrections, new prison construction is easily denied by referendum (Jacobs, 1983; Logan, 1990). Under voter pressure and legislative constraint, privatization provides an alternative to the traditional administrative solution. Comparatively, the modern capital market is putatively a far superior financing instrument that is faster, more responsive, and deficit-free. In 1996, seven management firms, such as Corrections Corporation of America and Wackenhut Corrections Corporation, were publicly owned and occupied 82% of the private corrections market (Thomas, et al., 1997). For governments in need of extra prison beds, lease agreements make the government payment a category of operational cost and avoid exposing the project to risky referenda.

Procedural inflexibility also pushes governments into contracting. Procedural management in the public sphere emphasizes equity, transparency, due process, and universal application of laws and regulations. While these values can promote efficiency by providing standard operating procedures, enhancing predictability, and curbing corruption, they may stymie innovations by imposing rigid constraints. Logan (1990) generalizes eight aspects of flexibility enhancement through prison privatization: more flexible programming, avoidance of capital budget limits, reduction of levels of bureaucracy, reduction of political intervention, avoidance of civil service constraints on personnel management, avoidance of bureaucratic self-perpetuation, promotion of specialization, and the shift of public administrators from rowing to steering.

## Economic Causes

Economic explanations focus on the cost efficiency of private prisons. The rising costs of maintaining prisoners, employing correctional personnel, meeting court-mandated prisoner rights, and providing rehabilitative programs, all lead to the rise of unit correctional costs and amplify the prison crisis. Reduction of per inmate correctional costs is in practice one of the strongest arguments for prison privatization, although the cost-efficiency virtue of private prisons is debatable. Empirical results are not consistent (ref. Chapter 2). Advocates of prison privatization claim an average of operating cost savings from 10 to 20 percent (Thomas, et al., 1997), while many deny the existence of systematic difference in operating cost between public and private prisons, or attribute cost reduction to service deterioration in private prisons (Donahue, 1988; GAO, 1996; Alexander, 2003).

Prison privatization is claimed to bring about cost savings in several ways. Private ownership matters (Hart et al., 1997). Driven by high-powered incentives to make profits, private firms care more about economic performance and take more efforts in maximizing efficiency. Market competition further pushes prison firms to explore their productivity margin. A private prison market also helps to break the borders between different correctional authorities and achieve economics of scale by pooling prisoners from different jurisdictions.[19] By having flexible payment arrangements, the government can avoid the sunk-cost dilemma. Governments can reduce the redundancy of prison staff and cells during non-peak periods by contracting out prisoners on a per diem rate base, with some risk sharing arrangements between the contractor and the government (McDonald et al., 2003). Private contractors have a more flexible labor market and can avoid many cost-inflating political, institutional, legal, and administrative constraints. Private prisons, according to these arguments, can more effectively make use of labor and technology.

---

[19] Only spec prisons may have this kind of effect. Sole-source private prisons, with their supply of prisoners limited to a single state, do not enjoy this advantage.

Nonetheless, major cost savings are often derived from labor cost reduction. Borjas (2003) argues that given working skills, the public sector has a relatively compressed wage distribution that has the "magnetic effect" to attract low-quality workers and crowd out high-skilled workers. Thus contracting out low-skill jobs to private firms can bring about cost savings. In 2000, a survey made by the Criminal Justice Institute (Camp and Camp, 2000) showed that the average entry level and maximum level salaries were $17,628 and $22,082 for correctional officers in private facilities, respectively 23 percent and 39 percent lower than their public counterparts. Yet, the reduced operating cost of private prisons does not necessarily lead to cost savings for governments. "Even if private-prison corporations succeed in cutting costs, there is unlikely to be sufficient competition in any given community to ensure that the savings result in diminished government budgets for corrections" (Donahue, 1988, p.2).

Besides these political, pragmatic and economic factors, intervention of federal courts in prison overcrowding is also deemed as important in influencing prison privatization. Since the 1960s federal courts began to give up the "hands-off doctrine" in dealing with prison administration and became active in establishing and protecting prisoner rights. Federal court orders were issued on prisons and State Department of Corrections (SDOC) to redress their "unconstitutional conditions," especially overcrowding. Such court orders placed prisons and SDOCs under unspecified terms of court supervision. Population caps were imposed, sometimes accompanied by fine. Prison administrators were left with the discretion to determine the means of compliance, but a failure to achieve compliance could lead to contempt orders, or court-appointed monitors (Levitt, 1996). While federal courts never challenged the constitutionality of private prisons, their orders may push states into SPP.

The above discussion is largely about the general causes of SPP. Placed in my theoretical framework of the privatization of core governmental functions, and placed in the historical development of SPP, these general causes can be organized in a meaningful way. Chapters 2 and 3 will organize and integrate these causes and Chapters 4, 5 and 6 will empirically examine their hypothesized influences on the magnitude of SPP. At this point, based on my discussion on the privatization of core functions and my identification of imprisonment as a core function, the above causes can be tentatively organized in the following ways: first, political factors and instrumental factors (including pragmatic and economic factors) may work simultaneously to influence the SPP decision. Second, politics may be the driving force of SPP, in both creating functional problems and shaping desirable solutions. Finally, the output of an SPP decision is reflected not only by the adoption of SPP, but also by the magnitude of SPP, which constitutes my research focus. These three points will be used to examine the empirical research at the state level that provides more specific perspectives on the causes of SPP.

## 1.7.2. Empirical Literature on the Prison Privatization Decision

Currently available empirical literature on the causes of SPP mainly includes three research projects by McDonald et al. (1998), Price (2002) and Nicholson-Crotty (2004). In Table 1.3, these three research projects are summarized. In Tables 1.4-1.7, I summarize findings of each research.

**Table 1.3. A summary of the three empirical research projects on SPP**

|  | McDonald et al. (1998) | Price (2002) | Nicholson-Crotty (2004) |
|---|---|---|---|
| Dependent variable | Existence of SPP contracts | Existence of private correctional facilities | Existence of SPP contracts |
| Research scope | 50 state governments, BOP, DC, Puerto Rico, and the US Virgin Islands | 50 states as geographical areas | 50 state governments |
| Data | Self-report (Survey) | Secondary | Secondary |
| Quantitative method | Ranking and sorting | Event history analysis | Logistic regression |
| Research period | 1997 | 1984-2000 | 1997-1998 |
| Cover both political and instrumental factors | Yes | Yes | Yes |
| Integrate political and instrumental factors | No | Yes | Yes |
| Differentiate political and instrumental factors | Yes | No | Yes |

**Table 1.4. Reported objectives of having SPP contracts, by 28 SPP authorities**

|  | Rank | | | | | No. (%) of |
|---|---|---|---|---|---|---|
|  | 1st | 2nd | 3rd | 4th | 5th-8th | states |
| Reducing overcrowding | 14 | 2 | 3 | 3 | 2 | 24 (86%) |
| Speed of acquiring beds | 2 | 9 | 4 | 1 | 4 | 21 (75%) |
| Gaining operational flexibility | 1 | 0 | 8 | 2 | 5 | 17 (61%) |
| Operational cost savings | 8 | 3 | 1 | 3 | 1 | 16 (57%) |
| Construction cost savings | 0 | 6 | 3 | 4 | 3 | 16 (57%) |
| Improving caliber of services | 1 | 0 | 0 | 1 | 9 | 12 (43%) |
| Reducing legal liability | 0 | 0 | 1 | 2 | 7 | 11 (39%) |
| Other | 3 | 2 | 0 | 0 | 1 | 6 (21%) |

Source: McDonald et al. (1998)

**Table 1.5. Reported reasons of not having SPP contracts, by 17 non-SPP authorities**

|  | No. of agencies |
|---|---|
| **Nonexistence of present or projected overcrowding** | 4 |
| **Labor concerns or labor opposition** | 4 |
| **Legal prohibitions** | 3 |
| **Issue in study or decision is pending** | 2 |
| **Cost savings not predicted** | 2 |
| **No extra funding** | 1 |
| **Concerns about accountability and quality of private management** | 1 |

Source: Adapted from McDonald et al. (1998)

According to the definition of SPP in Section 1.5, Table 1.3 shows that these three research projects adhere more or less strictly to SPP in establishing their research scope. McDonald et al. (1998) slightly extend the research scope to DC, Puerto Rico, and the US Virgin Islands, and the Bureau of Prisons (BOP). Price (2002) treats the state as a geographical concept and includes all facilities within the physical range of the state. Thus SPP in his research started from 1984 rather than 1986.[20] Nicholson-Crotty's (2004) unit of analysis is fully identical to mine: the 50 state governments. This table also shows that McDonald et al. investigate the causes of SPP by using self-reported data from governments about their motivations; while Price and Nicholson-Crotty use theory-driven empirical research to examine the hypothesized effects of influencing factors.

**Table 1.6. Explanatory models on the decision to privatize prisons, 1984-2000**

| | Expected influence | Economic Model | Ideological Model | Political Model | Complete model | Refined Model |
|---|---|---|---|---|---|---|
| **Economic Variables** | | | | | | |
| Correctional cost | + | - | | | - | |
| Per capita income | - | -* | | | - | -* |
| Tax capacity | - | +* | | | - | -* |
| Tax effort | + | +* | | | +* | -* |
| **Ideological Variables** | | | | | | |
| Liberal state ideology | - | | +* | | + | + |
| Liberal citizen ideology | - | | -* | | -* | -* |
| (Republican) governor | + | | + | | +* | |
| Republican legislature | + | | + | | + | - |
| **Political Variables** | | | | | | |
| Individual political culture | + | | | +* | + | +* |
| Prison capacity | + | | | + | + | |
| Neighbors | + | | | +* | + | + |
| Crime rate | + | | | +* | +* | +* |
| Pseudo R² | | .16 | .24 | .20 | .36 | .37 |
| Predictive efficiency | | .134 | .193 | .178 | .34 | .30 |

Source: Adapted from Price (2002).
* Significant at .05 level. +/- denotes the direction of influence.

---

[20] Ref. Section 1.4 for relevant information about the initiation of prison privatization at local, state, and federal levels.

Table 1.7. Explanatory factors of the maintenance of SPP contracts,
1997-1998

| Independent variable | Type of concern | Influences |
| --- | --- | --- |
| State ideology | Political | -* |
| Unionization | Political | + |
| Presence of enabling legislation | Political | +** |
| Gubernatorial power | Political | - |
| Tax and spending limits legislation | Instrumental | +* |
| Capital debt restriction | Instrumental | +** |
| Corrections as a percent of total spending | Instrumental | +** |
| Prison overcrowding | Instrumental | + |
| Chi-square | 46.79 ** | |
| Pseudo R-square | 0.27 | |

Source: Adapted from Nicholson-Crotty (2004).
* Significant at .05 level.
** Significant at .01 level. +/- denotes the direction of influence.

The major concern of this research is to reorganize political and instrumental factors in explaining SPP and to examine their influences on the magnitude of SPP. Considering the three points identified at the end of Section 1.7.1, Table 1.3 shows that none of these three research projects satisfy them all.

*(1) Coverage and Integration of Political and Instrumental Factors*
All three research projects show that both political and instrumental factors matter, yet in different ways. For one thing, the researchers have different indicators to represent political and instrumental factors. For example, Nicholson-Crotty chooses unionization as one of the indicators of the political environment but Price does not, while Price uses a set of indicators of states' fiscal capacity such as tax efforts and tax capacity but Nicholson-Crotty does not. For another, both Price and Nicholson-Crotty integrate these factors into the SPP decision, while the research of McDonald et al. shows an emphasis on instrumental objectives by contracting agencies and an emphasis on political constraints by non-contracting agencies.

## *(2) Differentiation in the Roles of Political and Instrumental Factors*

My discussion on the privatization of core functions entails a conscious examination of the possibly fundamental influences of the state's political environment. The researchers show different levels of emphasis on the uniqueness of political factors. Price combines political, economic, and ideological factors without hypothesizing their mutual relationship and his theoretical and empirical analyses fail to conclude whether a driving force exists. The research of McDonald et al. demonstrates that effects of political factors are mainly restrictive, while instrumental factors directly favor the making and maintenance of SPP contracts. Nicholson-Crotty consciously differentiates the effects of political and instrumental factors based on the traditional thought of a politics-administration dichotomy. Political factors are assumed important in determining the political feasibility in the adoption of SPP, reflected by the pro-SPP state legislation in his research, while instrumental factors are assumed critical in maintaining active SPP contracts. His research results show that political factors still matter in maintaining active SPP contracts. Overall, the current literature does not study SPP as the privatization of core functions and tends to juxtapose the explanations of different natures without distinguishing their relative role in the causal chain of SPP.

## *(3) Measurement of the SPP Decision*

According to Section 1.6, the empirical literature fails to clearly define, measure, and examine both research questions: the causality and the magnitude of SPP. Price measures the existence of private correctional facilities without differentiating the source of inmates. As a result, the contracting authorities may not be limited to state governments and the contracting state governments may not be the states where the facilities are located. Nicholson-Crotty measures whether states had an active SPP contract during 1997 and 1998, so his focus is the maintenance of SPP contracts, as is McDonald et al. His research is limited to in-state SPP contracts, failing to notice the fact that some states only export prisoners, although that accounts for only a small portion of the outsourced prisoners in the national total.

Consequently, this research differentiates itself by exploring the latter two aspects that are not well done by the existing literature: the different roles played by political and instrumental factors in causing SPP, and their influences on the magnitude of SPP. Further, this research intends to overcome some methodological imperfections in the empirical literature. For example, both Price and Nicholson-Crotty mainly use the general state features as explanatory variables, which can be used to analyze the privatization of a variety of services. Their relevance to SPP may not be so direct and may result in limited explanatory power. It is important to include some direct indicators of state prison systems, such as correctional cost efficiency and court orders on prisons. Also, the insignificant results of some putatively important factors, such as prison overcrowding and unionization, are not well interpreted. Nicholson-Crotty explains that the insignificance of overcrowding in his research may be due to the reduced pressure from federal courts since the passage of the *1996 Prisoner Litigation Reform Act*, yet no efforts are taken to quantify court pressures. He attributes the insignificance of unionization to the inaction of unions on SPP, yet it may in fact result from his model's misspecification.[21]

## 1.8. RECAPITULATION

This chapter identifies the conflict between the dominance of economics in the privatization literature and the emergence of the privatization of core functions. I argue that the privatization of core functions should be fundamentally explained by the logic of political economy, that is, politics *drives* the process and determines the relevance of instrumental concerns. This logic can be applied to SPP in analyzing its causes and magnitude. Before empirically testing the influences of political and instrumental factors on the magnitude of SPP in 2003, I will analyze in Chapters 2 and 3 the economic and political logics of SPP according to the analytical framework of the privatization of core governmental functions, with a purpose of identifying the causes of SPP.

---

[21] Nicholson-Crotty illustrates this by the coexistence of the super powerful California Corrections Peace Officers Association (CCPOA) and the second largest number of active correctional management contracts maintained by California. In contrast, Parenti (2003) argues that CCPOA "set the model and still leads the fight against privatization" (p.35). California has roughly the same number of state prisoners as Texas, 164,487 in 2003 (BJS, 2004a) that accounted for 13% of the national total, yet it only outsourced 3,507 state prisoners in 2003, accounting for 5% of the national total. Its SPP level was 2.1% in 2003. These facts may suggest that SPP in California is not really free of serious constraints from unions, especially in terms of the magnitude.

# Chapter 2

# THE ECONOMIC LOGIC OF
# STATE PRISON PRIVATIZATION

## INTRODUCTION

In this chapter I examine one major instrumental argument for state prison privatization (SPP): its cost savings to the government. I will first examine the markets and services of private prisons according to economic criteria. Then, I will examine the literature on the economic performance of private prisons. The purpose of this chapter is to examine whether SPP has the potential to bring about significant cost savings to governments.

## 2.1. PRIVATE STATE PRISONS: MARKET AND SERVICE

The market and the government are two different systems that have their own rules, goals, signs, and evaluation criteria. While the different scopes of service provision reflect the self-selection of these two systems according to their needs and advantages, they also further define the nature of the services they choose to provide. Both systems have formed specific conceptions, institutions, and values. The discussion on core functions shows that they are deeply embedded in the historical process of state building and integrated to the political governance system. Even if governments are willing to give up their monopoly of core functions in order to coopt the private sector, it is possible that the market can not really operate efficiently as it is assumed in delivering these services due to the noncompetitive market structure and the low measurability of services. Governments have to be the major buyer of these services and it is no doubt that the political and institutional environments will deeply intervene in market operation. As a result, it is highly possible that the so-called "market-based" government may distort the market order and contracting out may fail to realize its goals. These points are well reflected by the market and services of private prisons.

> *Noncompetitive market structure*: The development of a private prison market since 1986 shows a clear trend of concentration both through service market competition and capital market operation. According to the market classification scheme of Shepherd (1979) with a focus on measuring market shares and concentration, the private prison market is between a tight oligopoly and a dominant firm. From 1995-2001, among about 14 private management firms providing secure correctional services (including local jails and federal prisons), the two biggest ones, Corrections Corporation of America and Wackenhut Corrections Corporation, continued to occupied 75% of the market regarding prison capacity (BJS, 2004c). In 1997, 61 of the 91 federal and state contracts were held by them (McDonald et al., 1998). CCA is the dominant firm of this industry and controls 52% of the market share. Currently, CCA has 63 facilities in 20 states and Washington DC, contracting with all three federal corrections agencies, almost half of all states (namely most of the SPP states), and more than a dozen local municipalities. [1] Meanwhile, entry barrier between different states exists. "In some states, single firms are selected exclusively because of their political ties and are thus able to use monopoly rather than competitive pricing" (Crants, 1991, p53). These market situations may effectively limit competition.
> 
> *Lack of innovation*: Incarceration is a highly institutionalized field with many formal rules, regulations, and laws. This general environment may favor compliance rather than innovations (Meyer and Rowan, 1977), especially when the only buyer is the government. Besides, the labor-intensiveness of incarceration also makes technical innovations hard to apply (Donahue, 1988). An examination of the two-decade practice of SPP shows that private prisons strategically imitated public prisons in almost all aspects, including facility construction and daily operation. "…it appears that private vendors are usually not practicing

---

[1] See CCA web: http://www.correctionscorp.com/locationsmap.html

new ways of doing things. Instead, private vendors seem to see their task as one of refining processes already represented in the best practices of well-operated public systems" (Camp and Gaes, 2001, p.291). Such imitation, while serving the purpose of obtaining institutional appropriateness, tends to make the cost structure of private prisons resemble that of public prisons.

*Dilemma in service provision*: Privatization is often claimed as a way to correct the irresponsiveness of the public sector to consumer needs by introducing consumer choice (National Performance Review, 1993). The buying decisions made by governments or individual consumers signal their preferences, which can effectively motivate profit-driven contractors and induce desired services. Yet the incentive for profit may not always be transformed to quality-enhancing efforts. Prison privatization involves three parties: governments, prison firms, and prisoners. Privatization may offer a better position for governments, the buyer, in specifying services and in carrying out policy intentions more flexibly, yet may lead to a deterioration of the position of prisoners. Prison privatization does not change the relationship between service deliverers and recipients. Imprisonment is coercive and involuntary, with a purpose to induce negative utility. Prisoners do not have the option to exit, and as a disenfranchised group their voice is easily ignored. Yet, prison firms may benefit from less rehabilitative programs, cuts in prison services, proactive recording of prisoner violation of disciplines, harsher punishment, and high recidivism. Conflicts of interest between private prisons and prisoners may induce contractors to sacrifice prison services, both in the quantity and quality of services offered (Alexander, 2003).

*Low service measurability*: Low measurability in SPP creates incomplete contracts and may setback governments' goal to reduce cost while maintaining an acceptable quality of imprisonment through SPP. Imprisonment is a pure human service and does not produce material products. In other words, the products, the "rehabilitated" prisoners, are interactive and are not easily subject to objective measurement. When private prisons fail to meet the expectation of governments yet are not held accountable due to the lack of relevant contractual specifications, governments do not have the discretion to intervene in the operation of private prisons. This is the very reason why governments traditionally rely first on nonprofit and religious organizations in providing social and human services, counting on their sense of social responsibility (Handler, 1996). Due to the difficulty of performance measurement, monitoring and evaluation are often based on procedural indicators, such as the American Correctional Association (ACA) guidelines, that are easily manipulated by contractors (Hart et al., 1997). Yet despite the importance of monitoring, McDonald et al. (2003) disclose a problematic monitoring practice. In 1998, of the 89 prison contracts surveyed, 40% of in-state facilities had less than 20 hours per month of on-site monitoring. This figure rose to 90% for out-of-state facilities. For in-state facility monitoring, 63% of contract monitors had some training for the task, but only 14% of monitors for out-of-state facilities had such training. The coercive nature of imprisonment further amplifies the difficulty in measuring performance since feedback from prisoners will not be taken as a serious indicator of service quality. To enhance performance measurement means that governments have to make considerable investments on contract management.

*High asset specificity:* Highly specific investment creates bilateral monopoly and adds to the difficulty for governments to shift contractors, even when contractors are shown to be inferior. Correctional facilities are expensive and specialized in usage. Competition is effectively restricted by the sunk cost that sets entry barrier for potential competitors. For transactions with high asset specificity, long-term relational contract, or in-house production, is generally preferred to the market (Williamson, 1975). When private contractors invest on such assets, the risk-sharing mechanism often requires governments to guarantee a long-term supply of prisoners unless prison firms seriously breach their contractual obligations. There are also other kinds of transaction costs that make the shift of hundreds of prisoners from one facility to another the least desirable action for the government to take. SPP practice shows that entrenchment of private firms is the rule rather than an exception. The 1997 Abt survey shows that "among the 91 contracts that were active at year-end 1997, only 17 had been awarded following expiration of a previous contract. Of the 17, incumbency provides an overwhelming advantage: all but one of these were awarded to the incumbents" (McDonald et al., 2003, p.13). For the only exception, the facility was publicly owned and the bid was for its management. While the private prison market is already highly concentrated, high asset specificity further prohibts the freedom of governments in choosing contractors.

*Nonunion labor market:* Private prisons invariably use a nonunion work force to reduce labor costs. The following section will discuss the potential of cost savings by using a nonunion labor force. Section 3.2.3 discusses how this practice can be politically feasible. It is clear that cost savings from using nonunion work force have nothing to do with the claimed market superiority in management and innovation, but is fully a result of evading the binding norms on public organizations.

The above analysis suggests that SPP may not really have the potential to significantly outperform public prisons in operating efficiency, given service quality. Considering the economic arguments for prison privatization discussed in Section 1.7.1, economic theories are not consistent in supporting the privatization decision. At one hand, property theory and management theories may argue that private prisons can reduce operating cost; at another hand, imperfections of the market and the service suggest that generally recognized market virtues are not readily available and governments may not gain from the potential efficiency enhancement, even when it exists. Economic success of SPP depends on the extent to which governments are smart buyers and can skillfully manage the contracts. This makes cost savings a highly contingent outcome. In the following section, I examine the current literature that evaluates the performance of private prisons.

## 2.2. ECONOMIC PERFORMANCE OF PRIVATE STATE PRISONS

The empirical literature on the cost efficiency of private prisons has no conclusion on the cost savings from SPP. It is highly suspected that private prisons can save money for governments *and* simultaneously provide services no worse than public prisons.

Efficiency gain of prison privatization has two sources: facility construction and prison operation. Since SPP refers to the delegation of incarceration authority, the efficiency of private firms in facility construction is not really relevant to this point, although there is evidence that construction of facilities under SPP arrangement is a reliable source of cost savings.[2] This research discusses only the operating efficiency aspect. The prison industry is labor-intensive with labor expenditures accounting for the bulk of its operating costs. In 2001, salaries, wages, and benefits constituted 65% of state prison operating costs (BJS, 2004b). The basic way to reduce operating costs is to reduce compensation and staffing levels. Still, opportunities to realize these cost saving measures are limited because the compensation levels in public prisons are already low and significant reduction is unlikely to happen without significantly affecting staff quality. Table 2.1 demonstrates a positive relationship between compensation levels and staff quality.[3] Even when private prisons realize cost-efficiency by using cheap labor or by more efficient management, it is not guaranteed that governments would share this efficiency gain fairly with the stockholders and managers of private firms (Donahue, 1988).

**Table 2.1. Correctional officers in public and private prisons, 2000**

|  | Public | Private | Public/Private Ratio |
|---|---|---|---|
| Entry level salary (Average) | $23,002 | $17,628 | 1.3 |
| Maximum level salary (Average) | $36,328 | $22,082 | 1.7 |
| Annual Turnover rate (Average) | 16% | 52.2% | 0.3 |
| Pre-service training (Hours) | 250 | 153 | 1.6 |

Source: Adapted from Camp and Camp (2000).

Existing research on the operating efficiency of private prisons often compares per inmate operating cost (PIOC) between public and private prisons and is generalized by GAO (1996) and McDonald et al. (1998). A 1991 Texas Study compares four private, pre-release, minimum security prisons with

---

[2] Evidence is rich in concluding the superiority of private contractors to achieve cost saving and innovations while finishing prison construction significantly faster than governments, due mainly to the avoidance of numerous constraints on public actors (Yarden, 1994; Clark, 1998; Cripe, 1997).

[3] Compensation level is certainly only one of the factors that influence staff quality, but is an important one. SPP advocates may argue that compensation differences between public and private prisons are a result of the existence of unions in public prisons and has nothing to do with the quality of the staff. But it is hard to deny that better compensation attracts higher quality employees and induce better compliance to organizational goals and rules.

*hypothetical* public facilities in Texas and concludes a 14 to15% cost saving by using private prisons. A 1994 California Study compares three for-profit community correctional facilities, one privately run and two run by local governments. PIOC of the privately run facility is in the middle of the two operated by local governments. A 1995 Tennessee Study compares one private prison and two state-run prisons. There is little difference and PIOC of the private prison stays in the middle. A 1996 Washington Study reexamines the same three facilities of the 1995 Tennessee Study and concludes up to 6% cost savings from using private prisons. This study also compares the operating cost of three facilities in Louisiana, two private and one state-run, and finds that the public facility has the middle level of operating cost. Louisiana State in 1996 also made a study of two private prisons and one public prison that were all built by the state and had identical capacity and design. It shows that the two facilities operated by Corrections Corporation of America and Wackenhut Corrections Corporation saved 11.7 and 13.8 percent respectively. A 1996 Arizona study compares the PIOC of one private minimum security facility with the average PIOC of 15 state-run minimum security prisons and concludes a 17 percent savings from this private prison. These results are summarized in Figure 2.1 (Ref. Appendix A).

These studies are subject to many methodological deficiencies that make the evaluation less reliable (Camp and Gaes, 2001; McDonald et al., 1998). The first problem is the difficulty to measure the operating cost of private and public prisons.[4] There is ambiguity in cost calculation due to inconsistent accounting procedures, various cost dispersions, and the existence of overhead cost. Changes in criteria can easily lead to different results. Another problem is the difficulty in comparing the cost even when exact figures are available. It is necessary to control the property of prisoners, prison facilities, and service quality. Low cost may be a result of cherry-picking prisoner screening, better facility design, or cuts in rehabilitative programs, rather than improved management. The third problem is the involvement of temporal and geographical effects. Most research is cross-sectional or only covers a couple of years, thus is unable to catch larger trends. Meanwhile, most research is within one state whose specific context may not make the results generalizable.

---

[4] The cost of using private contractors includes the payment to contractors for services, cost of the contract management, and other costs associated with the facility's operation but covered by the government (McDonald, et al., 2003). The cost of using public prisons is even more fragmented and dispersed.

Despite these methodological concerns, there are three recognizable themes. First, existing research shows slight support for the cost-efficiency argument of private prisons. The results of empirical studies, generalized in Figure 2.1, offer support, although not consistent, for cost savings via private prisons. Nonetheless, the level of cost savings can not satisfy the 10-20% claim by SPP advocates. Another theme is the trend of homogenization between public and private prisons (Camp and Gaes, 2001) due to mutual learning and the gradual formation of an integrated correctional labor market. These changes result in diminishing returns on prison privatization (Austin and Coventry, 2001) and reduce the difference in prison operation. Finally, cost savings of SPP, if there are any, are mainly due to savings in labor cost (Alexander, 2003). Private prisons invariably use a nonunion labor force. A simple calculation makes this clear.

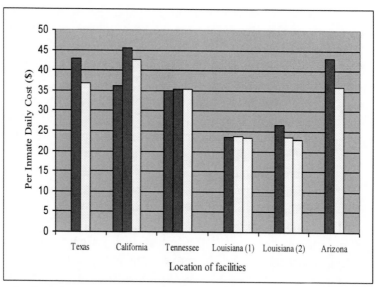

Source: GAO (1996), McDonald et al. (1998)
Note: Red bar denotes public prison. Yellow bar denotes private prison. The Louisiana (1) research was made by 1996 Washington Study; the Louisiana (2) research was made in the same year by Louisiana State. Ref. Appendix A for detailed information. The facilities of the 1995 Tennessee Study are reevaluated in the 1996 Washington Study, the results of which are not included.

Figure 2.1. Empirical research comparing per inmate operating cost between public and private prisons

If, according to table 2.1, the average compensation level of private prison staff is 20-30 percent lower than public prison staff, and the staffing level is 10-20 percent lower, and compensation constitutes 60-80 percent of all operating cost for comparable public prisons, then it is expected that private prisons will have 17-35 percent cost reduction through their use of nonunion labor. This cost savings will go to the prison managers, the stockholders, various constituencies of private prisons, and finally the government. Prison services are also an important place to reduce slack. Nelson (1998) concludes that the reduction in per-inmate medical expenditures and allocated state overhead costs constitutes the bulk of reported cost savings of private prisons in Tennessee. Greene (2003) and Alexander (2003) provide confirmatory evidence.

**Table 2.2. PIOC in 1996 and outsourced prisoners in 2003 for 10 states**

| States with highest PIOC | Annual cost ($) | Prisoners outsourced | States with lowest PIOC | Annual cost ($) | Prisoners outsourced |
|---|---|---|---|---|---|
| Minnesota | 37,800 | 0 | Alabama | 8,000 | 1698 |
| Rhode Island | 35,700 | 0 | Oklahoma | 10,600 | 6022 |
| Maine | 33,700 | 30 | Mississippi | 11,200 | 3463 |
| Alaska | 32,400 | 1386 | Texas | 12,200 | 16570 |
| Utah | 32,400 | 0 | Missouri | 12,800 | 0 |
| Average | 34,400 | 283 | | 10,960 | 5551 |

Source: BJS (1999, 2004a).

Further, despite the vagueness of the cost effectiveness of SPP due to the difficulty in comparison and to the newness of SPP, SPP practices in the US demonstrate, ironically, that SPP is more likely to happen in states with the least potential for cost reduction. Table 2.2 shows that the average PIOC for the 5 states with lowest PIOC was only one third of that of the 5 states with the highest PIOC. Yet prisoner outsourcing in the former 5 states accounted for 38% of the national total in 2003, compared to 2% for the latter 5 states. This clearly demonstrates the political segmentation of the prison market and suggests that efficiency concerns can hardly, independently explain SPP.

## 2.3. RECAPITULATION

This chapter examines the potential of private state prisons to save money for governments. Economic theories are inconsistent in claiming the cost efficiency of private prisons and provide little support the saving of public money from SPP. Despite the possible cost reduction in the operation of private prisons, the market and service of SPP make it hard for governments to benefit from it. A major source of cost efficiency enhancement through SPP is the use of nonunion workforces, which is not derived from a superior managerial capacity of private contractors or the pressure of market competition, but from a favorable political environment. The empirical literature shows that cost saving through SPP is limited and uncertain. Further, the ironical fact is that states with high unit correctional cost are inclined to refrain from SPP. As a result, the emphasis on cost savings is itself a thing to be explained.

# Chapter 3

# THE POLITICS OF STATE PRISON PRIVATIZATION

## INTRODUCTION

In this chapter I analyze two fundamental transformations in the governing philosophy of the US since the 1970s and their influences on prison privatization. The first transformation is the rise of conservatism in social control, while the second is the ascendancy of neoliberalism in economic restructuring policies. I will first, discuss these two policy trends and their relation to state prison privatization (SPP). Then, I will explain the development of SPP from a path-dependent view, highlighting the prominence of the south in SPP.

## 3.1. CONSERVATIVE SOCIAL CONTROL AND SPP

Crime control is an essential responsibility of governments, possibly its most basic function. Because of different beliefs as to the cause and control of crime, and even the definition of a crime, different political ideologies place different weight on the role of punishment in crime control. The liberal view tends to attribute the cause of crime to adverse social conditions and proposes curing both the "ill" criminals and the "ill" society, while the conservative view emphasizes the voluntary choice of the individuals and relies on punishment to regulate purposefully malign actors.

According to conservative social control philosophy, individuals should be responsible for their behavior. "Just deserts" should be strictly imposed on disobedient behaviors as a major way to maintain order. Inherently, conservatism inclines to use criminal justice policies to realize social control and maintain the order of (unequal) social distribution. As a result, in criminal justice areas, conservatism advocates a proactive, and even authoritative, role of the state in imposing punishment. While SPP in appearance has an effect or a purpose to shrink the state, its fundamental justification is rooted in the need of the state to expand in crime control.

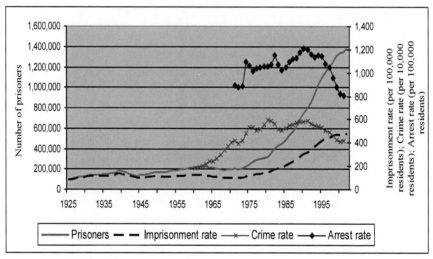

Source: (BJS, 2004c)
Notes: Crime rate has a per 10,000 residents base, while arrest rate and imprisonment rate have a per 100,000 residents base. US prisoners include both federal and state prisoners. Imprisonment rate does not cover jail inmates.

Figure 3.1. U.S. prisoners, crime rate, arrest rate, and imprisonment rate, 1925-2002.

### 3.1.1. The Rise of the US Custodial State

Since the 1970s, the rise of conservatism in criminal justice policies in the US created a modern "custodial state." Figure 3.1 shows that after decades of slow growth, US prisoners and imprisonment rate began to grow by leaps and bounds by the end of Nixon's presidency. During the same post-1975 period, neither crime nor arrest rates experienced similar increases. Rather, both of them decreased significantly since the late 1980s. Between 1990 and 2001, both decreased by about 30 percent.

The continuously diminishing gap between the crime/arrest rates and the imprisonment rate can only be explained by the toughened post-arrest government actions: imposition and administration of punishment. Before the 1970s there had been a period of liberal justice practice that pursued the rehabilitative goal of converting law breakers to law abiders. Indeterminate sentencing had been adopted by every state (Nagel, 1990). After that, the US justice system was gradually transformed to a determinate system (Mackenize, 2001). The rise of conservatism in crime control was reflected by systematic efforts to extend the scope of criminalization and to toughen law enforcement. *Anti-drug Abuse Acts* of 1986 and 1988 were passed to wage "war on crime" by criminalizing drug offenses, which accounted for 55.5 percent of federal prisoners in 2001 (BJS, 2003b). The *Comprehensive Crime Control Act of 1984* established mandatory minimum sentences for certain crimes, especially violent crimes and drug offenses. Three-strike laws were adopted by many states to cope with recidivism. Release decisions were also made rigorous. By 2000, 29 states had adopted the federal truth-in-sentencing standards that require mandatory release according to statutory provisions (BJS, 2004c), with an intention to reduce discretionary release of offenders by parole boards. As a result, from 1990 to 1998, there were a decline of release rate of state prisoners from 37% to 31% and meanwhile an increase in the mean time served from 22 months to 28 months (BJS, 2000a). These policies highlight the shift of crime control to the justice model that is rooted in conservative philosophy.

The intensification of the judicial-political control began in the Nixon era. It was initially a political response to the civil disobedience in the 1960s, an age of Civil Rights and anti-war movements. While some fruits of these movements were legally acknowledged under a liberal federal government through a series of Supreme Court decisions and federal laws such as the *1964 Civil Rights Act*, the political opposition on the right chose to demonize the new left, the civil rights activists, and to connect liberal reforms with crime and moral decay (Wood, 2003). Such a tendency to blame the liberals, the federal bureaucracy, and to promote state and local rights through law-and-order strategies was represented by the Alabama governor and presidential candidate George Wallace, whose conservative stance was adopted by the Nixon, and especially, the Reagan administrations. This political resistance used the strategy of heavily utilizing criminal justice policies, which were mainly the jurisdiction of states, to offset the liberal federal policies. Then, California Governor Reagan was active in enforcing criminal laws against campus radicals and anti-war protestors engaging in disruptive behavior. In 1969, he sent 2,200 National Guard soldiers to take over the Berkeley campus.

Beyond short-term responses to political rebellion in the 1960s, "get tough on crime" became a strategy to gain political support by utilizing the fear of crime, especially violent crime. As part of a political debate, the harsh advocacy of "getting tough" often exaggerates crime control problems, and creates more fear and demand for draconian methods of crime control. *General Social Surveys 1972-2002* (National Opinion Research Center, 2003) shows that despite the unprecedented expansion of the US criminal justice system and declining crime rates, from 1973 until 2002, the average percentage of people thinking that the government spends "too little" on crime control and dealing with drug addiction were 66% and 60% respectively, with education 61%, improvement of conditions for blacks 32%, and welfare 19%. "Get tough on crime" distinguished itself as a political imperative for politicians thirsty-for-votes and fearful of risking their careers by being perceived as taking a soft stance on crime. The 8 year Clinton Administration still saw a 43 percent increase in prison inmates (413,143), compared to the 139 percent increase in the previous 12 years of Reagan and Bush Administrations (530,303).

## 3.1.2. SPP as a Constitutive Element of the Custodial State

The new custodial state makes three requirements on public prison systems: punishment-centered corrections, flexibility in punishment, and a large inmate population. These requirements on corrections greatly reduce the political and moral resistance to SPP and stimulate the demand for SPP.

The custodial state promotes a return to retribution in corrections. Correctional philosophy under the justice model deemphasizes the rehabilitative goal but increases its punitive color. Prisoners are not treated as victims of adverse social conditions but as immoral citizens. Concerns for prisoner welfare and civil rights protection are replaced by an emphasis on security, control, and coercion. [1] "Supermax" prisons grew popular. Rehabilitative concerns for the psychological and economic conditions of prisoners are marginalized, for example, by putting them in prisons far way

---

[1] The passage of *1996 Prisoner Litigation Reform Act* is a legislative check on the increasing amount of prisoner litigations that are frequently "frivolous" and on the micro-management of state prison systems by federal courts (Belbot, 2004).

from their home communities.[2] Since prisoners do not fall under the *Fair Labor Standards Act*, minimum wage and benefits laws do not apply to them. The commercial use of their labor is once again justified.[3] Many states allow commercial entities to use prison facilities and labor for manufacturing purposes, For example, in 1995, Oregon voters passed a constitutional amendment requiring all its state inmates to be involved in work programs. It is estimated by the Correctional Industries Association that in 2000, 30 percent of America's inmate population worked to create nearly $9 billion in sales for private business like McDonald's and K-mart (Overbeck, 1997).

Accompanying the alienation of prisoners was the deprofessionalization of corrections. Professional values are highly dependent on the socioeconomic status of the clients served by the profession. The rise of correctional professionalism in the 1960s was a byproduct of the Civil Rights Movement and the increased protection of prisoners' rights. Under the rehabilitative model of corrections, professionals were trusted to monitor the rehabilitation of prisoners, make flexible classifications, give good time credit, assign rehabilitative programs, and determine the time of release. Beginning in the 1970s, there was a systematic transfer of power from correctional systems to courts and from criminal justice systems to politicians. Discretion, especially semi-adjudication authority of correctional professionals, was either eliminated or restricted. These new changes tended to bureaucratize correctional staff by requiring more compliance to written documents and standards. In 2000, only 14% of staff in state prisons was classified as professional, technical, or educational, compared to 36% of federal correctional employees (BJS, 2003a).

SPP is in accord with these changes in prison culture and operation. Private prisons are punishment-centered and benefit from high (growth of) inmate populations, longer terms, high recidivism, and less rehabilitative spending. The private prison industry is very active in lobbying for toughened crime control. Also, professionalization level in private prisons is similar to that of public state prisons. In 2000, it was 17%, slightly higher than public state prisons but far less than federal prisons (BJS, 2003a).

The custodial state also requires more flexibility in incarceration. Governments face a risk of being accountable when correctional systems are punishment-centered and violate prisoners' rights. Contracting out can soften

---

[2] For example, in 2000, about 50 percent of Texas prisoners were sentenced in four counties, while only 3.7 percent of them were incarcerated there.
[3] The *1979 Justice Systems Improvement Act* set a waiver on the *1940 Sumners-Ashurst Act*'s restrictions on interstate commerce of convict-made goods.

the lines of legal accountability by converting the pure state-prisoner relationship to a more blurred firm-prisoner relationship, which may hedge governments against accountability claims by commercial means. There are impressive stories about the unaccountable contracting situations created by SPP. In February 2005, the New York Times published a series titled "Harsh Medicine" that reported the death and suicide of prisoners due to inadequate health care provided by Prison Health Services, the largest US for-profit provider of prisoner medical care (Zielbauer, 2005). Iraq's 2004 Abu Ghraib prison scandal was its international counterpart whereby the Pentagon contracted with private contractors to seek intelligence through draconian methods of interrogation. Full prison privatization is even more radical in insulating governments from responsibilities. Although governments in theory hold ultimate accountability for unconstitutional conditions in private prisons that are in fact acting on the behalf of the state (Gilmour and Jensen, 1998; Shichor, 1995), contracting out elongates the chain of accountability and sets a buffer, if not a firewall, against liability claims toward the government. Some scholars argue that government privatizes prisons with the purpose of reducing prisoner litigation against it and avoiding financial liability. "Private prison companies typically offer contracts in which they indemnify the government against the total cost of any harm resulting from the operation of their facilities" (Logan, 1990, p.191). Despite often insufficient insurance coverage by private firms, the exposure of government to liability, nevertheless, is usually reduced by prison privatization (McDonald, et al., 1998).

Finally, the custodial state incarcerates a large population that may exceed its prison capacity. Criminal justice systems are composed of police, courts, and prisons that constitute a consecutive process of criminal screening, filtering and correction. Among them, police and prisons are both labor-sensitive and relatively inelastic, while the "output" of courts has a high sensitivity to policy changes. Changes in sentencing criteria will directly influence the number of new prisoners and the length of their terms. Figure 3.1 discloses that while crime/arrest rates declined, toughened sentencing policies led to the increase of imprisonment rate. This is the fundamental cause of prison overcrowding and the financial difficulty of corrections. Consequently, the correctional segment constitutes a bottleneck to the expansion of criminal justice systems. As a response, from 1980 until 1999, the proportion of state correctional expenditures in state criminal justice expenditures increased from 49 to 60 percent. This relative increase was still insufficient to digest the output from courts. Clearly, political changes create these functional dilemmas in correctional systems, and these functional problems require a trade-off between the state monopoly of prisons and prison privatization.

While the first priority of law-and-order politicians was to convince their constituencies of their mettle by the number of arrests and convictions made, it was of secondary importance as to how the convicted would be imprisoned. The less weight they assigned to corrections and their unwillingness to pay the cost, the more likely they were to favor the option of external supply. Meanwhile, under the punitive prison culture, the moral sin of prisoners was emphasized, leading also to an emphasis on punishment rather than rehabilitation. Harsh punishment was simply moral and paying a lot to sustain prisoners was regarded as wasteful. Hence, profit-making private prisons should be desirable if they saved money. The option of prison privatization was favored by the legal environment. It was rare for a state to ban SPP legislatively. Federal courts also refrained from denying the constitutionality of prison privatization; instead, federal court orders were imposed on states to reduce overcrowding. The necessity of a state monopoly for incarcerating state prisoners was weakened. Becker and Mackelprang (1990) disclose that the validity for contracting out state prisoners, as evaluated by state legislators, is higher than the validity of contracting out tax collection or regulatory policy-drafting. It is natural to go beyond service-contracting to full prison privatization.

While direct administration of punishment by the state is reduced in a relative sense by the participation of private partners, SPP serves well the desire of a custodial state to reform corrections while enlarging and deepening punishment. The survival strategy of private prisons goes hand-in-hand with a conservative crime control philosophy. By strategically imitating public prisons and eagerly acquiring symbolic resources in the institutional environment, private firms manage to reduce political barriers by shifting attention to pragmatic and economic issues.

# 3.2. NEOLIBERAL ECONOMIC POLICIES AND SPP

Punishment is profitable. This is especially true under conservative social control policies. The prison boom since the 1970s created a prison industrial complex (Hallinan, 2001; Schlosser, 1998; Wood, 2003). Unprecedented amounts of government spending created vested commercial and political interests in the continuous expansion of prison systems. From 1986 to 2001, total state government spending on corrections increased from $15.5 billion to $38.2 billion in 2001 constant dollars, and expenditures on state prisons increased from $11.7 billion to 29.4 billion. These expenditures create great opportunities for businesses and employment. A 2004 report shows that the proportion of counties with at least one prison in 10 states increased from 13 percent in 1979 to 31 percent in 2000 (Lawrence and Travis, 2004).[4] Sixty two counties had 10% or more of their population in prison, with 2 of them, one in Florida and one in Texas, having 30% or more of their population in prison (ibid). From an emphasis on punishment, there derived a complex chain of vested political-economic interests. Prison unions, legislators from rural and poor areas, prison construction, service, and management firms, and local governments are all included in a prison construction advocacy coalition.

As a result, the share of correctional expenditures in state budgets grew steadily from 2.5 to 4.1 percent between 1982 and 2001 for the whole nation (ref. Section 4.2.1), making corrections a target of neoliberal economic policies. In the following section, I will discuss how neoliberal economic policies reshaped US correctional systems that led to SPP.

### 3.2.1. Neoliberal Economic Philosophy

In the 1970s the old governance doctrines in the US, characterized by Keynesian economic policies, liberal social policies and social democratic welfare policies were seriously challenged. Oil shocks of the 1970s generated inflation, high interest rates, and an economic slump. This stagnation ended the continuous economic prosperity and growth since World War II, reshaped ideas about the marketplace, and altered the political ecology of the US. These economic changes created a congenial environment for emerging neoliberal economic policies, which peaked with Ronald Reagan's rise to presidency, and has remained in the mainstream of American economic policies. The pro-market ideational foundation of neoliberalism was built on economic theories such as public choice. At the core of neoliberalism is a set of economic principles that redefine the state-society relationship with consistent support for a market-based economy and state:

---

[4] These states experienced the largest growth in the number of prisons during the 1980s and 1990s, including California, Colorado, Florida, Georgia, Illinois, Michigan, Missouri, New York, Ohio, and Texas.

1. *Rule of the market*: The freedom of capital, goods and services, and labor is the foundation of economic order, development, and wealth distribution. Markets are efficient. A minimal state should refrain from doing things other than maintaining market order and providing pure public goods.
2. *Deregulation*: The state should reduce regulations that distort self-regulating markets.
3. *Privatization*: The state should rely on the private sector to provide and deliver social and governmental services.
4. *Retrenchment*: The state should reduce taxation and spending, and shed functions to individuals and markets.
5. *Decentralization*: The state should enlarge the role of low-level governments in providing and financing public goods.[5]

These doctrines, incorporated in Reaganomics, define the appropriate scope of the government and the appropriate ways of enacting governmental duties, and require an essential and market-based state. Underlying neoliberalism is a rationalized destruction of protective state-based social mechanisms. It reverses the century-long efforts of the labor movement to protect workers from the uncertainty of self-regulating markets, boldly relieves the government of its social responsibilities, and proposes to run the state like a business. The Reagan Administration continued to cut income taxes, shed social programs to state and local governments, deregulate the economy, liberalize trade, and privatize government enterprises and services. Consequently, the trend of reducing income inequality between World War II and the 1970s was reversed.[6] An age of high unemployment returned like that of 1975 and was only interrupted during the Clinton Administration. High unemployment restrained the wage level and increased business profits. Since the late 1970s, the real value of federal minimum wage has fallen considerably,[7] accompanied by declining unemployment benefits and cuts in job and social welfare programs. Trade liberalization also brought about extra pressure on the domestic labor market by inducing increased outsourcing of

---

[5] The shedding of functions to state or local governments may, ironically, bring about the centralization of policy making to the federal government that makes policies and seeks universal application for these policies by using intergovernmental grants.
[6] During the 1980s and 1990s, income inequality widened significantly not just between the low-income families and the high-income families, but also between the middle-class families and the top-income families (Bernstein, et al., 2000).
[7] According to Bernstein et al. (2000), the value of the minimum wage in 2000 was 18 percent below its average value during the late 1970s.

manufacturing and service jobs to cheap-labor countries (Ali, 2004). These pro-capital restructuring efforts effectively induced vast investment in technological and service innovations. With the coming of the "new economy" in the 1990s, the American economy did get out of its doldrums.

It is worth noticing that neoliberalism achieved fruition in reforming governmental services mainly through structural retrenchment. Expenditures on national defense and basic economic infrastructure continuously expanded, while some social programs such as Aid to Families with Dependent Children (AFDC) and housing policies, were cut, shrunk, or failed to grow (Pierson, 1994). Meanwhile, the retrenchment in federal expenditures was offset by the expansion of state and local governments. During 1981-1989, the percentage of federal expenditures in GDP decreased by 0.53 percent to be 22.5 percent, yet the percentage of total government expenditures in GDP increased by 0.3 percent to be 32.38 percent (Hyman, 1997). While total expenditures never shrank, retrenchment through the offloading of governmental services appears to have been achieved to different extents across different service areas.

## 3.2.2. Correctional Reforms under Economic Neoliberalism

Neoliberal reforms of public correctional systems seek to transfer correction-related economic interests to the private sector and reduce their costs by optimizing the efficiency of correctional operation.

From the neoliberal perspective, it is wrong to build a large correctional-bureaucratic system, while it is right to let private firms have a larger share in prison service production. The discretion to distribute the newly-appropriated public expenditures on corrections provides a perfect opportunity for the government to implement correctional reforms. Besides other related economic restructuring goals, such as the creation of large-scale low-paid jobs and the transfer of public funds from urban to rural areas, it is an obligation of the neoliberal state to transfer to the private sector the increasing correction-related public expenditures. Besides, privatization provides a good opportunity for politicians to reward or break up political alliances, vitiate correctional unions, and create an integrated market of correctional labor.

Neoliberal correctional reform also mandates squeezing welfare out of the correctional systems and reducing correctional costs. A tenet of neoliberalism is to rely on private markets to gain efficiency. A minimum state can not be achieved if it is not efficient. The goal of cost saving is made more relevant considering the budgetary pressure on corrections. Because labor costs constitute the bulk of prison operating expenditures, significant cost reduction requires the marketization of correctional labor. Yet, this reform intention is seriously impeded by the existence of strong correctional unions. From 1983 to 2003, union membership nationally decreased from 20.1 percent to 12.9 percent (Bureau of Labor Statistics, 2004), while it increased for correctional officers from 44 percent to 51 percent (Hirsch and Macpherson, 2004).[8] Although recent developments in prison privatization have forced correctional unions to readjust their role and their relationship with governments (Camp and Gaes, 2001), full privatization of existing prisons is unlikely.

Neoliberalism takes two indirect paths in bringing correctional employees back to market discipline. One way is to contract out prison services. Although the federal government sets stipulations on the wage rate of workers employed by federal contractors,[9] contractors often have no such obligations when doing business with state governments. Although service-contracting is common and raises relatively few legal disputes, it nonetheless faces strong objection from unions since it may directly overtake the work of correctional officers. Another way is via full prison privatization in the form of extended privatization. Imprisonment, accompanied by all prison services, can be outsourced to private facilities.

### 3.2.3. SPP as the Ideal-Type of Neoliberal Correctional Reform

Private state prisons fully embody the neoliberal requirements on correction and impose pressure on the reform of public prisons. Secure private prisons are all run by for-profit firms organized according to modern enterprise institutions and most of them are publicly owned (Thomas, et al., 1997). Their operation is market-driven with a goal of profit-making. Private prisons have an almost entirely nonunion workforce (Camp and Gaes, 2001). The ambition of private prisons to reduce the bid price for government contracts, to pay prison managers handsomely, and to create profits for investors, is to a great extent based on labor cost reduction. Correctional employees in private prisons are not represented by public correctional unions.

---

[8] Most states have national unions, such as the American Federation of State, County, and Municipal Employees, as their affiliated unions, while some states have statewide, independent unions such as the California Corrections Peace Officers Association.

[9] The *Service Contract Act of 1965* obligates contractors of the federal government to use the wage rates that are based on prevailing practice in the local labor market and are set by the US Department of Labor.

The establishment of collective bargaining needs to start anew at the signature gathering and election phase.[10] Organizing a union lacks political support, especially when private prisons provide job opportunities for residents in economically depressed communities. In these areas, residents and local politicians are more interested in job opportunities than job security and compensation. This geographical-political strategy in choosing facility location enables private prisons to get both cheap labor and strong constituencies. The opposition of correctional unions to the private prison industry also makes it difficult for them to get involved in the unionization of private prison employees. As a result, low-paid staff with a high-turnover rate is widely used in private prisons, as Table 2.1 shows. Despite the quality-reducing effect of low compensation, in 2000, average prisoner-staff ratio of private prisons was 3.8, 29 percent higher than that of public state prisons (BJS, 2003a). Meanwhile, average income disparity (the ratio of annual income between prison administrator and entry level correctional employees) grew to be 3.08 in 1999, with a maximum value of 5.13 for the Great Plains Correctional Facility, Oklahoma (Camp and Camp, 2000).

### 3.3. A Path-Dependent View on SPP

Viewing SPP from a historical perspective helps to organize the above arguments. History matters. The essential argument of path dependence is that "path dependence is a way to narrow conceptually the choice set and link decision making through time" (Pierson, 2000, p.256). The path-dependence perspective entails tracing the causes of the patterned difference among states in SPP at t period by looking at t-1 period, or an even earlier historical juncture. Figure 3.2 shows that within the US, the south has disproportionately high levels of incarceration, prison privatization, and conviction-based disenfranchisement; the northeast and midwest have disproportionately lower levels in these aspects; and the west is in the middle.[11]

---

[10] The *National Labor Relations Act* (NLRA) mandates that if a formerly public facility with unionized labor is privatized, and if the private operator hires a substantial and representative component of the former work force, then the union must be recognized automatically. In the case of SPP, most private prisons are new facilities and are not subject to the concern of hiring an organized labor force. Staff in private prisons must either form their own union or join existing unions.

[11] These four regions are culturally and historically defined. In this research, the states that comprise these regions are based on the classification scheme by the Bureau of Justice

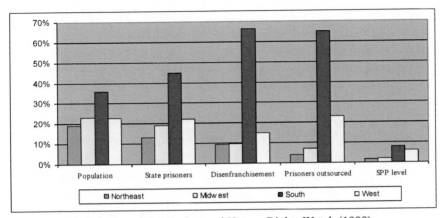

Source: BJS (2004), Sentencing Project and Human Rights Watch (1998).
Note: The last group of bars shows the regional SPP level of every region. These bars do not add up to 1.

Figure 3.2. The regional share of population, state prisoners, and outsourced state prisoners in 2003; the regional share of disenfranchised citizens in 1996; and the regional SPP level in 2003.

Such differences in judicial-political control and SPP were largely determined by the early history of the US. A typical comparison can be made between two extremes, the south and the north (mainly northeastern and some midwest states). Before the Civil War, the north and the south had already formed distinctly different paths of political and economic development. The north was chasing the first industrial revolution and expanding industrial-capitalist systems. In contrast, the south was an agricultural and race-based slavery economy, whose socioeconomic foundation was seriously threatened by the liberal north. The northern Union Army defeated the political rebellion of the south in the Civil War and broke down slavery, but failed to shake apart the structure of social power and implant northern capitalist institutions in the south. Shortly after, the second industrial revolution mainly benefited northern states that had already developed proper industrial, technical, and market infrastructures. The labor movement grew as industrial and social protection mechanisms were gradually established. Compared to northern states, southern states were poor, undereducated, mainly agricultural and rural, and with serious racial discrimination. Conservative ideology found its most favorable

Statistics. This composition may not be fully compatible with the cultural concept of these regions.

climate in the south. Historically, the south created the prototype for both conservative social control and neoliberal economic policies.

The custodial state model was originally a "southern strategy" (Wood, 2003; Parenti, 2001) to maintain the racial order by criminalizing, imprisoning, and disenfranchising blacks. After the Civil War and the passage of the 15th amendment to the Constitution, the newly obtained voting rights of blacks constituted a potentially serious challenge to the old racial order. Once the era of Reconstruction was over, southern states made state laws to resist federal policies. The punitive nature of laws in traditional societies was continued, strengthened, and used to serve as a tool of racial control. "Between 1890 and 1910, many southern states tailored their criminal disenfranchisement laws, along with other voting qualifications, to increase the effect of these laws on black citizens" (Shapiro, 1993, p3). Even today most southern states still widely impose conviction-based disenfranchisement on ex-felons, prisoners, probationers and parolees. The intensity of judicial-political control in 1996 was 0.86 in southern states, two times that of northern-midwestern states and one and a half times that of western states.[12] Southern states also have tougher laws and law enforcement policies. In 1971 when the liberal period of criminal justice policies was to end, the incarceration rate in the south was already 220 percent higher than that in the northeast (Wood, 2003). Since the 1970s this southern practice has became a national trend. During 1980 and 2002, the increase in incarceration rates in the south was exceeded by the other three regions, yet the absolute growth of incarceration rates for the south was still the highest (BJS, 2004c).

Meanwhile, the economic reliance on slavery and agriculture in the south produced the prototype of neoliberal economic operation and philosophy. Southern states, in general, had relatively low taxes on capital, a low level of public services, and substantially low wage levels. The lack of modern industries, enmity to the labor movement, and a low level of urbanization restricted the development of labor unions and social protective mechanisms. This pattern survived the modernization process of the south. During 1977 and 2003, the average unionization level of employed wage and salary workers in southern states was 13.4%, compared to 21% in the northeast (Hirsch and Macpherson, 2004). Segregation between public and private labor markets is

---

[12] The calculation of the intensity of judicial-political control is according to the frequency of the use of conviction-based disenfranchisement on four parallel categories of people: ex-felons, prisoners, probationers and parolees. For instance, if there are two states and only one of them disenfranchises ex-felons, then the score will be 0.125 (1/8). Data source is Sentencing Project and Human Rights Watch (1998), ref. Appendix B.

relatively low. In this sense, contracting out governmental services in these states may not save as much money as in northeastern states where labor is more expensive. However, the low level of unionization also reduces the political resistance to privatization. These factors, combined with the traditionally important prison economy in the south, provide congenial social background for prison privatization.

The historical features of the south determined that it would become the birthplace and headquarters of prison privatization. In 2003, there were only three non-SPP southern states: Arkansas, Delaware, and West Virginia. Among them, Delaware and West Virginia are both border states and neither of them was a member state of the Confederacy. Their connection to the south, as a cultural concept, is not so intimate.

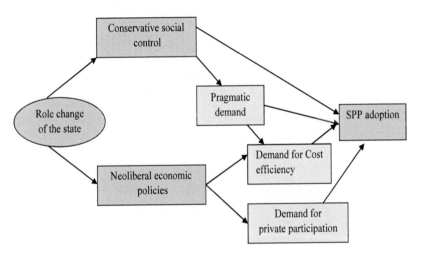

Figure 3.3. The political economy logic of the adoption of SPP.

## 3.4. A GENERALIZATION OF THE POLITICAL LOGIC OF SPP

Figure 3.3 generalizes the above analysis of the causality of SPP. It is a path-diagram and shows the process that finally leads to the initiation of SPP in the US, namely the adoption of SPP. Figure 3.3 identifies politics as the fundamental driving force. Both conservative social control and neoliberalism have independent influences on SPP. Yet they are not independent. They were rooted in the conservative political tradition and were deeply involved in the transformation of US public governance since the 1970s. It is not incidental that Ronald Reagan promised to both "get tough on crime" and "get government off our backs, out of our pockets".[13] Among these two political streams, the rise of conservatism in social control constitute an expansion theme that creates a pragmatic demand for SPP and removes the political and moral barriers toward SPP by reshaping the nature of imprisonment. The pragmatic demand for extra prison cells directly favors private partnerships, and the budgetary pressure also favors SPP for cost savings and the avoidance of capital investment. The rise of neoliberalism constitutes a retrenchment theme that mandates the transfer of correction-related economic benefits to the private sector and pursues cost efficiency. As a result, while instrumental factors may be more direct in influencing the adoption of SPP, the fundamental driving force is politics, especially the punitive bandwagon of crime control.

## 3.5. RECAPITULATION

In this chapter I develop the logic of political economy in SPP by exploring the driving forces of SPP. Conservative social control and neoliberal economic policies provide basic support for SPP. They create the instrumental problems, thus the demand for private participation, and they reduce the political and morale resistance to private prisons. SPP serves the conscious self-adjustment of the state without, explicitly, challenging existing political structures and institutions. Both conservative social control and neoliberal economic policies have their roots in the south. The path dependence in social conditions and public policies makes SPP a natural development in the south. The following chapters analyze empirically the variation of SPP levels among the states in 2003.

---

[13] Quoted from Ronald Reagan's speech at a Montana Republican Party rally in Great Falls. http://www.reagan.utexas.edu/resource/speeches/1982/102882c.htm

# Chapter 4

# AN EMPIRICAL EXPLORATION
# OF THE MAGNITUDE OF SPP

## INTRODUCTION

In this chapter I analyze the variation among states in their magnitude of SPP, or in another words, in their different levels of reliance on the private sector. I will identify, discuss, and operationalize the explanatory variables, and make hypotheses on their effects. Based on the data structure, I will identify the appropriate statistical model.

## 4.1. MEASUREMENT OF THE MAGNITUDE OF SPP

In this research I empirically research the variation of the magnitude of SPP among the states in 2003. The magnitude of SPP reflects the objective level of a state's reliance on private contractors. According to Section 1.6, it is measured by the percentage of state prisoners under private custody. The existing research (ref. Section 1.7.2) only measures the existence of SPP contracts while ignoring the different levels of states' engagement in SPP. Section 1.6 has discussed the advantages of examining the magnitude of SPP compared to the adoption of SPP or the existence of SPP contracts. It is worth stating that the magnitude of SPP contains two kinds of information: whether the state outsources prisoners, and what percentage of prisoners is outsourced. A positive value means that the state has outsourced prisoners at a certain level.

Bureau of Justice Statistics (BJS) reports annually the percentage of prisoners outsourced to private prisons by the 50 states since 1999. I will use the most recent 2003 data as the dependent variable of this research (ref. Appendix C). Figure 4.1 shows a highly right-skewed distribution of SPP levels in 2003.[1] Twenty (40%) states were non-SPP states with a value of 0 in 2003; 20 (40%) SPP states had SPP levels less than 10 percent but larger than 0; the remaining 10 states (20%) had SPP levels larger than 10 percent. The data are censored (ref. Sections 4.4 and 4.5). Table 4.1 shows the ten states with SPP levels greater than 10 percent in 2003. The SPP level does not necessarily reflect the role of the state in the national SPP market. Texas is the national SPP leader with the largest number of outsourced prisoner and the largest import of prisoners. In 2003 it outsourced 16,570 prisoners, 175% higher than Oklahoma that was next to it in number, yet it only had an SPP level of 9.9 percent due to its huge prison population. Comparatively, New Mexico had the highest level of SPP in 2003 yet its number of prisoners outsourced was only 16% of that of Texas. Besides, it was a net-export state.

Geographically, Figure 4.2 indicates that southern and western states are most active in SPP. Comparatively, western SPP states are most aggressive in having high levels of SPP, while southern SPP states are most aggressive in maintaining a large number of outsourced prisoners. Seven of the ten states with an SPP level greater than 10% were western states in 2003, yet while 69% of westerns states outsourced prisoners in 2003, its counterpart in the south was 81%.

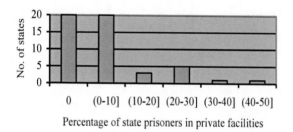

0       (0-10]   (10-20]  (20-30]  (30-40]  (40-50]

Percentage of state prisoners in private facilities

Source: BJS (2004a).

Figure 4.1. Distribution of the magnitude of SPP across states, 2003.

---

[1] Skewness characterizes the degree of asymmetry of a distribution around its mean. The direction of the skewness depends upon the location of the extreme values. If the extreme values are in the larger observations, the mean will be the measure of location most greatly distorted toward the upward direction. Since the mean exceeds the median and the mode, such distribution is said to be positive-skewed or right-skewed.

**Table 4.1. States with SPP levels greater than 10% in 2003**

| States | Prisoners outsourced | SPP level (%) |
|---|---|---|
| Mississippi | 3,463 | 14.9 |
| Colorado | 3,013 | 15.3 |
| Tennessee | 5,049 | 19.9 |
| Idaho | 1,267 | 21.5 |
| Hawaii | 1,478 | 25.4 |
| Wyoming | 493 | 26.3 |
| Oklahoma | 6,022 | 26.4 |
| Montana | 1,059 | 29.3 |
| Alaska | 1,386 | 30.6 |
| New Mexico | 2,751 | 44.2 |

Source: BJS (2004a).

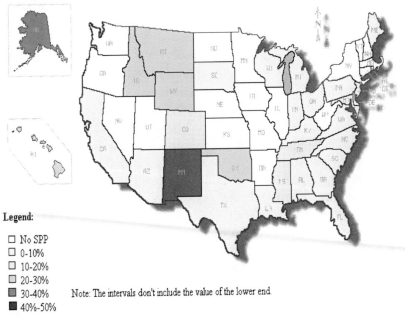

Legend:

□ No SPP
□ 0-10%
□ 10-20%
□ 20-30%
■ 30-40%    Note: The intervals don't include the value of the lower end.
■ 40%-50%

Source: BJS (2004a)

Figure 4.2. Geographical distribution of SPP levels, 2003.

## 4.2. ASSUMPTION, MODELS, DECISION FACTORS, AND HYPOTHESES

Chapters 2 and 3 focus on exploring the causal chain of SPP and suggest that SPP is fundamentally driven by conservative social control and neoliberal economic policies, which create functional problems for correctional systems and also shape desirable solutions to these problems. This logic of political economy suggests that both political and instrumental factors may work to influence the states' choice of the appropriate levels of SPP. None of them may provide a complete explanation. For example, politics may fail to explain why some liberal northeastern states, like New Jersey, had relatively high levels of SPP in 2003; while highly conservative southern states, such as Arkansas, had a level of 0.[2] Fully relying on instrumental explanations may be incomplete, or wrong. For example, there is a negative relationship between per inmate operating cost and the magnitude of SPP. While my theoretical framework and the existing empirical literature unanimously support the importance of both political and instrumental factors in causing SPP, it is quite reasonable to assume that these factors also work continuously to determine the magnitude of SPP, although the influence of these factors on the magnitude may not be identical to their influence on the adoption of SPP. Consequently, to account for the variation in the magnitude of SPP among the 50 states, it is necessary to look at both political and instrumental factors.

The rationale for examining both political and instrumental factors is also based on the multiple decision-makers of SPP decisions. McDonald et al. (1998) identify three types of initiators of SPP through a survey in 1997, which includes state legislatures, governors, and SDOC administrators. A 1996 survey on SPP also identifies lobbyists for several private companies (Virginia) and community-based groups (Oklahoma) as originating the initiative of prison privatization (National Institute of Corrections, 1996). While in most cases SDOCs make contracts with private firms,[3] such action in

---

[2] Arkansas has the lowest score of state policy liberalism, indicating a highly conservative state political environment. It once had an SPP contract in 1997 (McDonald, et al., 1998).

[3] There is one exception due to the inter-governmental conflicts in the attitudes toward SPP in Florida. In 1985 Florida legislature passed Chapter 944.105 to authorize the Florida Department of Corrections (FDC) to "enter into contracts with private vendors for the provision of the operation and maintenance of correctional facilities and the supervision of inmates." Yet no action was taken until 1993 when the state legislature established a separate agency, the Florida Privatization Commission (FPC), to implement its *1993 Correctional Privatization Act*. As a result, both FDC and FPC made SPP contracts after 1993 (McDonald et al., 2003).

fact reflects decision making by a wide decision network composed of various SPP advocates and opponents.

In this research, I assume a comprehensive rationality of the SPP decision. The magnitude of SPP is determined by a process involving both politicians and administrators with both of them being subject to political and instrumental concerns. Figure 4.3 shows the codetermination of political and instrumental factors on the magnitude of SPP. States face the simultaneous influences of political and instrumental factors as far as the magnitude of SPP is concerned.

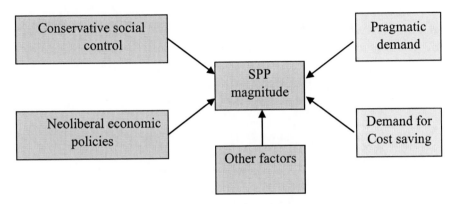

Figure 4.3. Influencing factors on the magnitude of SPP.

In order to examine the explanatory power of instrumental and political factors, I examine two Tobit models. The reduced model has only instrumental factors, while the complete model has both instrumental and political factors. The temporal effect (years of SPP practice) and the number of federal court orders will be included in both models since their influences can not be classified as political or instrumental. The number of state prisoners in 2003 will be used as a control variable in both models. The reduced model is used to illustrate the capacity of instrumental factors in independently explaining the magnitude of SPP, while the complete model combines instrumental and political factors. Section 4.5 will introduce the statistical model and the specification of the reduced and the complete models.

## 4.2.1. Variables of Instrumental Concerns

Instrumental factors set pragmatic and economic incentives and constraints on SPP (ref. Section 1.7.1 for a detailed explanation of these factors).

Prison overcrowding is by far the most broadly recognized causes of SPP. From 1985 to 2002, the number of state prisoners jumped by twofold from 451,812 to 1,226,175, dwarfing the rapid increase in the capacity of state prisons (BJS, 2004c). In 1995, the maximum overcrowding rate of state prison systems reached 177% (Ohio), with a national mean of 114% (BJS, 2003a). This variable reflects the level of incapacity of the states to imprison prisoners and the level of unconstitutional prison conditions. It is highly expected that SDOCs may turn to the private market to reduce such demand-supply gaps.

Hypothesis 1: State governments with a high level of overcrowding tend to increase their magnitude of SPP.

Budget crisis may be another cause that pushes states into SPP. From 1982 to 1990, the proportion of state correctional expenditures in the total expenditures of states' justice systems increased from 52% to 61% (BJS, 2004c). In 1999, this proportion declined from its peak of 64% in 1997 to 61%. Similarly, from 1982 to 1990 the proportion of state correctional expenditures in the total current expenditures of the states increased from 2.5% to 3.8% before the growth stagnated. In 2001 this proportion was 4.2%.[4] These changes demonstrate that states adjusted the distribution of their fiscal resources to favor correctional expenditures. Yet, over time it grew more difficult for corrections to take advantage of the potential fiscal capacity of states. Those states that have spent a large share of their total budget on corrections may face more difficulty in increasing it in the future and may be more inclined to privatize prisons.

Meanwhile, since the late 1970s, many states introduced tax and spending limits legislation (TSL) as a response to taxpayer revolts and budge deficits. Budgetary rules under TSL impose restrictions on how much taxes and/or expenditures can increase from one year to the next. Since the enactment of Proposition 13 in California in 1978, 27 of the 50 states have established some kind of TSL legislation. There is empirical evidence suggesting that "well designed TSL imposes fiscal discipline on elected officials" (Poulson, 2004,

---

[4] The data are based on BJS (2004c) and Baker (2003).

p.2) and can effectively constrain the growth of governments. Reliance on SPP may be attractive if the fiscal pressures from TSL are at least equally distributed on correctional and other expenditures.

Hypothesis 2: State governments that spend a large proportion of their state budgets on corrections tend to increase their magnitude of SPP.

Hypothesis 3: State governments with TSL tend to have a high level of SPP.

Budget crisis does not simply result from the increasing number of prisoners, but also from the increasing per inmate operating cost (PIOC). In fiscal year 2001, PIOC of state prisons averaged $22,650, with a maximum $44,379 (Maine) and a minimum $8,128 (Alabama) (BJS, 2004b). It is intuitively reasonable to believe that the higher the per inmate correctional cost, the higher the potential for state governments to gain cost savings through SPP. Cost savings from SPP constitute one basic argument for SPP. Many states make certain levels of cost savings a legal precondition for prison privatization. For example, the Texas legislature sets 10% cost reduction as the precondition for contracting out prisoners, while it is 7% for Florida (McDonald et al., 2003).

Hypothesis 4: State governments with high PIOC tend to increase their magnitude of SPP.

## 4.2.2. Political Variables

Political factors are those that set political incentives and constraints on SPP.

Under US federalism, vast areas of governance are reserved for state governments. State differences matter in policy making and implementation (Fenton, 1957; Elazar, 1966; Sharkansky, 1970; Erikson et al., 1987). State prisoners and state prisons are mostly a state policy issue. State correctional policy making reflects the popular ideology and public opinion of the state (Erikson et al., 1989), and shows the behavioral patterns of state decision making agencies. These factors show the internalized political tendency of states and are relatively stable over time. Theoretically, if a state is more conservative in its political environment, it is more likely to have a strong preference for a nonintrusive government and for neoliberal economic policies, and thus is potentially more favorable to prison privatization.

Hypothesis 5:  State governments whose political environment is highly conservative tend to have a high level of SPP.


Regional identity has historically been important in the US as a source of political identity, policy innovation, and policy adoption. This is certainly true for criminal justice policies as well. In Chapter 3, I argue that the south is locked in a tradition of a heavy use of punishment and a high rate of incarceration, whereas the northeast has tendencies in the opposite direction. Historically, the west was more akin to the south while the midwest was more akin to the northeast in these aspects. Besides the style of crime control, regional effects also include two other effects: one that is relatively static and another that is relatively dynamic. Together, they tend to homogenize states in the same region. The relatively static regional effect is the existence of an ideological identity regarding the general role of government in dealing with social and economic issues. This may create a similar need and acceptability for SPP. The relatively dynamic effect is the policy learning and diffusion among states in specific policy fields (Gary, 1973; Berry and Berry, 1999), which first happens in contiguous and ideologically similar states. Normative and mimetic processes of isomorphism crosses state borders (DiMaggio and Powell, 1983). Existence of SPP in nearby states better justifies its legitimacy than a trend in far-away states. Geographical contiguity also creates instrumental advantages.

### Table 4.2. Regional SPP leaders in 2000

|                        | Custody count | Jurisdiction count | Import |
|------------------------|---------------|--------------------|--------|
| Texas (South)          | 18,009        | 13,985             | 4,024  |
| Tennessee (South)      | 4,974         | 3,510              | 1,464  |
| California (West)      | 5,895         | 4,547              | 1,348  |
| Oklahoma (West)        | 8,502         | 6,931              | 1,571  |
| Wisconsin (Midwest)    | 0             | 4,337              | 0      |
| Ohio (Midwest)         | 2,470         | 1,918              | 552    |
| New Jersey (Northeast) | 2,608         | 2,498              | 110    |

Source: BJS (2001, 2003a).
Note: The assumption to calculate the import total is that states will first outsource prisoners to within-state facilities.

Outsourcing prisoners to private facilities in nearby states saves money and reduces contract-monitoring difficulties. In combination, ideology and policy transfer may reinforce regional effects.

Comparatively, southern and western states, in general, initiated SPP far earlier than the other two regions,[5] and both regions have strong SPP leaders.[6] Table 4.2 shows that the four SPP leaders in the south and west counted for 40% of outsourced state prisoners and 52% of the supply of private prison cells, providing a net import of 8,407. Texas alone contributed 4,024 prison cells for other states, constituting 23-32 percent of the interstate private prison market.[7] Such absorption effects will first benefit nearby states and entice them to export prisoners. Comparatively, major SPP leaders in the midwest and the northeast had only a small scale of SPP, and contributed very little to the interstate private prison market. Recognizing the hesitance of the northeast to employ punishment-centered corrections and its lack of SPP leaders, the impact of regional difference is hypothesized as:

Hypothesis 6: Southern, western and midwestern state governments tend to have a high level of SPP compared to northeastern states.

Unions are the major opponents of SPP (Logan, 1990). "The most important direct check on the expansion of private gulags is the growing political muscle of unionized prison guards" (Parenti, 2003, p34). The first prison employee union was established in 1956 (Duffee, 1983). Collective bargaining coverage in public prison systems grew fast due largely to the enactment of comprehensive labor laws (Freeman and Ichniowski, 1988). In 2003, while nationally only 12.9 percent of wage and salary workers were union workers, 36.1 percent of workers of protective service occupations[8] were unionized, only slightly less than the education, training, and library occupational sectors (Bureau of Labor Statistics, 2004). In 2000, according to the Current Population Survey, there were 356,207 state government prison

---

[5] In 2003, southern states had an average of 8 years of SPP practice, while this was 9 for western states, 5 for midwest states, and only 2 for northeastern states.

[6] An SPP leader in this research refers to a state that outsources a large number of state prisoners.

[7] In 2000, there are 17 net export states with 12,656 state prisoners imported. There are 22 net import states with 17,154 state prisoners imported. This 4,498 difference in number between the net import and export is mainly a result of the temporal difference between the data sources.

[8] Protective service workers include police officers, sheriff's deputies, criminal investigators, correctional officers, jailers, detectives, security guards, and firefighters.

employees. [9] Among them, 53.8% were union members and 58.4% were covered by collective bargaining agreements. Among the American Federation of Labor & Congress of Industrial Organizations (AFL-CIO) unions, American Federation of State, County, and Municipal Employees is the most powerful one by representing 100,000 publicly-employed prison guards and making intensive efforts to resist prison privatization.

Unlike many other governmental agencies whose constituencies are their service recipients, the major constituencies of public correctional agencies are their custodial employees (Clear and Cole, 1990). This makes correctional unions especially powerful in protecting employees' job security and compensation packages. The fast expansion of the public prison systems also strengthened the political power of correctional officers and their unions. A high degree of unionization, in theory, is a distortion to the labor market with a cost-increasing effect (Hirsch and Addison, 1986; Lewis, 1988) and constitutes the very justification for the entry of private prisons that use nonunion workers. A former CEO of Corrections Corporation of America (CCA) says in a straightforward way that "efficient labor is precluded in public facilities in several states by unionized labor. Union contracts tend to increase wage costs and promote unjustified job security" (Crants, 1991, p.53). In reality, unions are most active in opposing SPP. For example, the Rhode Island correctional officers' union contract contained a no-subcontracting provision that prohibits the privatization of correctional facilities (National Institute of Corrections, 1996). Unions pushed forward the legislation of a one-year moratorium on new privatization of prisons or jails in Pennsylvania (Logan, 1990). The Tennessee State Employees Association failed the two attempts of CCA to take over the state's entire prisons system in 1997 and 1998 (Parenti, 2003).

Hypothesis 7:   State governments with a low unionization level in their correctional systems tend to increase their magnitude of SPP.

Professionalism is another factor that may influence correctional organizations' response to privatization. Characteristics of professionalism are well recognized (Hughes, 1965; Mosher, 1968; Ammons and King, 1984), but theories about professionalism are less developed (Frendreis and Vertz, 1988). On the whole, autonomy, ethical codes, technical expertise, associational

---

[9] The estimated number of state correctional employees in 2000 by BJS (2003a) is 372,976, a little different to the Current Population Survey data.

membership, professional standards and accreditation are indicators of professionalism. They set entry barriers and reserve power, reputation, and handsome pay for the insiders. Professional authority and hierarchical authority may not mutually conflict (Toren, 1976). American correctional systems have experienced a transformation to greater professionalism by which the professional employees obtain a larger share in the number of prison staff and more authority.[10] Interestingly, SPP may not impose serious threats to professionalism. As pointed out earlier, due to the use of a strategy of imitation, private prisons have a slightly higher proportion of professional employees than state public prisons. Private prisons are also more enthusiastic to obtain American Correctional Association (ACA) accreditation. SPP, under the general environment of correctional deprofessionalization, may not necessarily harm professional values. Rather, professional practice, for example the payment standards, may penetrate public correctional systems. Professionals and high level managers may benefit from a more flexible labor market and receive better compensation packages. While private prisons widely use lower-paid staff, the compensation structure tends to favor the professional staff.

Hypothesis 8:   State governments with high professionalism in their correctional systems tend to increase their magnitude of SPP.

## 4.2.3. Other Explanatory Variables

The temporal effect refers to the institutionalization effect that cumulates support for SPP over time and makes it irreversible. Political and technical constraints, combined with people's limited capacity to calculate, make policy-making naturally incremental, and resistant to comprehensive changes (Wildavsky, 1965; Lindblom, 1959). Theory of path dependence argues that large set-up cost, learning effects and coordination effects, and adaptive expectations create increasing returns and build a stable path, the cost of reversion of which increases as the path extends over time (Pierson, 2000). Further, policy innovations that are initially introduced for their functional benefits may, in the long run, penetrate the formal institutional systems and gain a life that no longer relies on their instrumental values (Tolbert and

---

[10] Professional employees include counselors, psychologists, social workers, chaplains, medical staff, and educational staff.

Zucker, 1999). SPP practices in the US also exhibit this effect. SPP cultivates its constituencies. New prison facilities bring important economic opportunities to local communities, making local economies a hostage to their continuous operation and prosperity (for example, ref. Parenti [2003], p.33). While public correctional officials and employees typically are not allowed to lobby, representatives of private firms do not have this restriction. Besides, private prisons have large set-up costs by building single-purpose facilities. The public-private partnership under SPP generally requires risk sharing between a government and a contractor. Long-term contracts are the rule rather than the exception. As a result, entrenchment of private firms is often unavoidable. Governments are not really free to terminate contracts or to shift partners even if they are fully justified in doing so. The 140% increase in the number of private prisons and the 445% growth of the rated capacity of private prisons from 1995 to 2000 (BJS, 2003a) indicates that the practice of SPP may reinforce the momentum for its growth over time.

Hypothesis 9: State governments with a long duration of SPP practice tend to increase their magnitude of SPP.

Correctional systems directly face demands and pressures from their task environment (Thompson, 1967), among which federal courts are an important one. Federal courts became an intrusive regulator of correctional systems since the 1974 *Wolff v. McDonnell* case.[11] "Prison matters usually come to the attention of the courts through class-action suits on behalf of all prisoners or through writs of habeas corpus for individual inmates filed under the *Civil Rights Act of 1971*, 42 USC. § 1983" (Bowker, 1983, p.1226). In 1995, a total of 456 federal and state prisons (including private prisons) were under court orders or consent decrees, and 229 of them covering 29 states were to limit prisoner populations (BJS, 2003a). Pressure on correctional systems grew as the operation of prisons increasingly fell under the supervision of the courts.[12] SPP provides an option to relieve the pressure of overcrowding.

Hypothesis 10: State governments under serious pressure from federal courts tend to increase their magnitude of SPP.

---

[11] Scholars may have different opinion on the starting point of this policy tendency. For example, Belbot (2004) identifies the 1964 Cooper v. Pate as opening the floodgates to federal courts.

[12] Court intervention spans a wide scope including crowding, visiting, mail and telephone privileges, religious policies, accommodation of disabled, medical services, library services, food service/nutrition, recreation, counseling programs, education, and many others.

## 4.2.4. Control Variable

With the same number of prisoners outsourced, states with larger prison populations will have a low magnitude of SPP. For states that have a small prison population, for example 1,680 prisoners for Wyoming in 2000, a single SPP contract may lead to a relatively high level of SPP. To account for the possible distortion in SPP levels due to the vast differences in prison populations, I will include the number of state prisoners in 2003 as a control variable.

## 4.3. Operationalization and Analysis of the Explanatory Variables

According to Section 4.2 and based on the available data, the explanatory variables are operationalized and briefly analyzed. Table 4.3 shows the descriptive information for all the variables. The data are further examined by using two different but related classification schemes. Table 4.4 compares the means of the independent variables for three groups of states: the 10 significant SPP states with an SPP level higher than 10%, the 20 modest SPP states with an SPP level between 0 and 10%, and the 20 non-SPP states that did not outsource prisoners in 2003. Table 4.5 groups the states according to every independent variable (IV) in ascending order and divides the states into two groups with equal number of states (25) if the IV is a continuous variable. For TSL and regional dummy variables, the division is based on their dichotomous values. This table examines the average magnitude of SPP for the two groups of states. These two tables show that state political culture, regional difference, unionization, and temporal effects have consistent and expected effects across the groups of states. Other factors are more or less inconsistent or unexpected. The examination of the descriptive statistics provides information complementary to the regression analysis of Chapter 5. Appendix D shows the correlation matrix between the IVs, and Appendix E provides the multicollinearity diagnostics.

*Overcrowding* (H1): Overcrowding is represented by the percent of rated capacity occupied for all state prisons in 1995. The data are from the *Census of State and Federal Correctional Facilities, 2000* (BJS, 2003a). Table 4.4 shows that non-SPP states (105%) have only a very slightly less overcrowding level than modest SPP states (108%) and significant SPP states (106%). Table 4.5 shows that the 25 states with relatively low overcrowding (97%) have an average SPP level 3.3% higher than the 25 states with relatively high overcrowding (116%). The univariate information does not suggest a positive influence of overcrowding on the magnitude of SPP.

*Proportion of correctional expenditures* (H2): Proportion of correctional expenditures (PCE) is measured by the share of state correctional expenditures in the total state government direct expenditures in 1996. The data are from the *Sourcebook of Criminal Justice Statistics, 1999* (BJS, 2000b). Table 4.4 shows that modest SPP states have an average PCE level (4.3) significantly higher than non-SPP states (3), while significant SPP states only have a slightly larger PCE level (3.3) than non-SPP states. Table 4.5 shows that the 25 states with relatively high PCE have an average SPP level 1.7% higher (insignificant) that the 25 states with a relatively low PCE. PCE in general shows a positive influence on SPP.

*Tax and spending limits* (H3): Tax and spending limits legislation (TSL) is a dummy variable. It is measured so that the value of "1" represents the existence of state laws in 1995 that established a cap on the growth of revenues or expenditures. The data are from National Conference of State Legislatures (2004). Table 4.4 shows that there is no difference in TSL between non-SPP states (0.45) and modest SPP states (0.45), yet significant SPP states have a significantly higher level of TSL (0.8). Table 4.5 shows that the 26 TSL states have an average SPP level 3.76 percent higher (insignificant) than the other 24 states. The descriptive information also suggests a positive influence of TSL on SPP.

*Per inmate operating cost* (H4): Per inmate operating cost (PIOC) measures the unit cost of state corrections in fiscal year 1996. The prisoner count is based on jurisdiction count so that it covers prisoners outsourced under SPP contracts. The data are from the *State Prison Expenditures, 1996* (BJS, 1999). Table 4.4 shows that non-SPP states have an average PIOC (24.2) significantly higher than modest SPP states (20.3) and also higher (insignificant) than significant SPP states (20.7). Table 4.5 also shows that the 25 low-cost states have an average PIOC 41 percent lower than high-cost states, but have an average SPP level 1.1 percent higher than the latter. The descriptive information generally shows a negative influence of PIOC on SPP.

*State policy liberalism* (H5): The composite policy liberalism scores developed by Erikson et al. (1993) are used to represent the general state-level liberal-conservative tendencies in policy-making. This indicator sums the standardized scores of the states on 8 state policy issues including education, Medicaid, Aid to Families with Dependent Children (AFDC), consumer protection, criminal justice, legalized gambling, equal rights amendment, and tax progressivity.[13] High and positive scores represent a high level of liberalism in the state's political environment. Hawaii and Alaska are not included in their research and will be assigned the median value of western states.[14] Table 4.4 shows that the three groups show continuous decrease from liberal 0.41, to slightly conservative -0.18, to conservative -0.55, indicating a consistent influence on SPP. Both modest SPP and significant SPP states have significantly higher average magnitude of SPP than non-SPP states. Table 4.5 shows that relatively conservative states have an average SPP level of 10.98%, significantly higher than 2.93% for relatively liberal states. This suggests that a state's political environment has a strong influence on the magnitude of SPP.

*Regional difference*: (H6): This research makes the regional difference a dummy variable with northeast as the base of comparison and examines the effect of being a midwestern, southern or western state on SPP. Regions are defined according to the classification by the Bureau of Criminal Justice Statistics. Table 4.4 shows that northeastern and midwestern states are unlikely to have modest level of SPP, and it is significantly unlikely for them to have an SPP level greater than 10%. Southern states are very likely to have a modest SPP level, while western states are very likely to have an SPP level greater than 10%. Table 4.5 shows that northeastern and midwestern have a significantly lower SPP level than remaining states, while western states have a significantly higher SPP level than remaining states. Southern states have a slightly higher SPP level than the remaining states.

---

[13] These policy issues have different measuring methods. For example, education measures public educational spending per pupil, Medicaid and AFDC measure the scope of eligibility, and consumer protection measures the responsiveness of states to the consumer movement by making legislation on unit pricing, open dating, drug advertising, etc.

[14] Major properties of the Tobit results will not change if Hawaii and Alaska are removed from the dataset. Yet removing them is not desirable due to the reduction of data size and due to the large SPP values of these two states.

*Unionization level*: (H7): The unionization levels of state public prison systems are not available. I will follow Nicholson-Crotty's (2004) suit to use the unionization level (the level of collective bargaining coverage) of public sectors of every state in 1995 as a substitute. This may be appropriate since the unionization efforts and achievements are in general consistent across public sectors in individual states. The data are from the online database of Current Population Survey made available by the Bureau of Labor Statistics. The descriptive information of unionization has an identical pattern to that of state policy liberalism. In Table 4.4, the respective average values for the three groups show a consistent change: 49:37:32. Table 4.5 shows that the 25 states with a low level of unionization have an average SPP level 4.8 percent higher than the other 25 states. All t-tests in these two tables are significant.

*Professionalism* (H8): Professionalism is measured by the proportion of professional staff in the correctional staff of state prison systems. Professionals are those classified as professional, technical, and educational staff. The only available data are the year 2000 data provided by the *Census of State and Federal Correctional Facilities, 2000* (BJS, 2003a). From 1995 to 2000, the proportion of professional prison staff nationwide (including federal prison staff) stayed at 16 percent (BJS, 2003a). This suggests that the state-level data in 2000 may well reflect the reality between 1995 and 2000. Table 4.4 shows that significant SPP states have a higher professionalism score than non-SPP states, but modest SPP states do not. Table 4.5 shows that states with higher correctional professionalism scores have higher SPP levels. There is no significant result in t tests comparisons.

*Years* (H9): The years variable is the number of years that states had been outsourcing prisoners during the last two decades. It is equal to $t_{last} - t_1 + 1$. $t_{last}$ refers to the last year of SPP practice, in most cases 2003. $t_1$ refers to the first year of prisoner outsourcing.[15] There are no directly available data. However, multiple sources can be used to obtain the data.[16] The data show that among the 20 non-SPP states, 10 states

---

[15] This research only considers the recent practice of SPP, which started in 1986 in Kentucky. So $t_{last}$ or $t_1$ should have a value no smaller than 1986 and no larger than 2003.
[16] These sources include McDonald et al. (1998), Camp and Camp (2000), and BJS (1996, 2004a).

never adopted SPP up to 2003.[17] Another 10 states did not outsource prisoners in 2003 but had done so sometime in the past (ref. Section 1.6). The positive average value of non-SPP states shows that SPP can be used as a short-term tool for some states. Table 4.4 shows a very consistent effect of years on SPP: 2:9:10. Table 4.5 shows that the 25 states with a relatively long SPP practice have an average SPP level 12 percent higher than the remaining states. All the t-tests for the years variable are significant.

*Court order* (H10): The number of 1995 court orders requiring state prisons to limit inmate population is used. In 1995, excluding the 6 DC prisons, 223 state prisons were under court order to limit inmate population, including 210 public state prisons and 13 private state prisons. The data are from the *Census of State and Federal Correctional Facilities, 2000* (BJS, 2003a). Table 4.4 shows that there is only significant difference in court orders between non-SPP states and modest SPP states (1.5:8.4). Table 4.5 shows no significant different between states with fewer court orders and states with more court orders.

*State prisoners*: The number of state prisoners under the jurisdiction of state governments in 2003 is used as a control variable. The data are from the *Prisoners in 2003* (BJS, 2004a). The high end of state prisoner populations, Texas, had 166,911 prisoners, 135 times that of the low end, North Dakota. Tables 4.4 and 4.5 show a pattern of descriptive statistics similar to that of the Court order variable. Modest SPP states have significantly larger prisoner populations than non-SPP states, yet significant SPP states do not. There is no significant difference between the 25 states with relatively small prisoner populations and another 25 states. Still, the descriptive statistics do not demonstrate a consistent pattern of influence.

---

[17] These 10 states include Connecticut, Massachusetts, New Hampshire, New York, Rhode Island, Vermont, Illinois, Iowa, Nebraska, and West Virginia.

**Table 4.3. Descriptive statistics of the dependent and independent variables**

| | Min | Max | Mean | Std deviation | Expected effect | Measurement |
|---|---|---|---|---|---|---|
| DV: SPP level 2003 (%) | 0 | 44.2 | 7 | 10.47 | | Percentage of state prisoners outsourced in 2003 |
| IVs: | | | | | | |
| Pragmatic and economic variables: Xi | | | | | | |
| Overcrowding 95 (%) | 85 | 177 | 107 | 15.76 | + | No. of State prisoners /rated capacity of state prisons including private prisons |
| PCE 96 (%) | 1 | 6.5 | 3.6 | 1.3 | + | Correctional expenditure/total direct expenditure of state government |
| TSL 95 | 0 | 1 | 0.52 | 0.51 | + | Existence of TSL equals 1, else 0 |
| PIOC 96 ($1000) | 7.99 | 37.8 | 21.9 | 7.25 | + | Per inmate operating cost for all state prisoners |
| Political variables: Xp | | | | | | |
| State policy liberalism | -1.54 | 2.12 | -0.03 | 0.96 | - | Liberal-conservative tendency in state policy making. High scores indicate high liberalism. |
| Region        Midwest | 0 | 1 | 0.24 | 0.43 | + | |
|                   South | 0 | 1 | 0.32 | 0.47 | + | 1 if the state is in that region, else 0 |
|                   West | 0 | 1 | 0.26 | 0.44 | + | |
| Unionization 1995 (%) | 10.8 | 74.2 | 40.9 | 17.81 | - | Collective bargaining coverage of state public sectors |
| Professionalism 2000 (%) | 2.9 | 23 | 14.7 | 4.34 | + | Professional, technical and educational staff/total correctional employees |
| Other explanatory variables: Xo | | | | | | |
| Years | 0 | 18 | 6.4 | 5.26 | + | Duration of SPP practice since 1986 |
| Court orders 95 | 0 | 58 | 4.5 | 9.89 | + | Number of court orders on state prisons to limit overcrowding |
| Control variable: Xc | | | | | | |
| State prisoners 2003 | 1.24 | 166.9 | 25.93 | 33.65 | - | The number of state prisoners, in thousand |

**Table 4.4. Mean, standard deviation (SD), and t-test of the IVs**

| | Non-SPP states: SPP = 0 | Modest SPP states: 0 < SPP < 10% | | Significant SPP states: SPP > 10% | |
|---|---|---|---|---|---|
| | Mean and SD | Mean and SD | t-value | Mean and SD | t-value |
| Overcrowding 95 (%) | 105 (12.33) | 108 (19.84) | 0.54 | 106 (13.85) | 0.27 |
| PCE 96 (%) | 3 (0.92) | 4.3 (1.49) | 3.32*** | 3.3 (0.85) | 0.96 |
| TSL 95 | 0.45 (0.51) | 0.45 (0.51) | 0 | 0.8 (0.42) | 1.89* |
| PIOC 96 ($1000) | 24.2 (7.54) | 20.3 (6.82) | -1.7* | 20.7 (6.99) | -1.22 |
| State policy liberalism | 0.41 (0.86) | -0.18 (1.04) | -1.96* | -0.55 (0.66) | -3.08*** |
| Northeast | 0.3 (0.47) | 0.15 (0.44) | -1.04 | 0 (0) | -2.85*** |
| Midwest | 0.35 (0.48) | 0.25 (0.44) | -0.68 | 0 (0) | -2.24** |
| South | 0.15 (0.36) | 0.5 (0.51) | 2.48** | 0.3 (0.48) | 0.95 |
| West | 0.2 (0.41) | 0.1 (0.3) | -0.87 | 0.7 (0.48) | 2.97*** |
| Unionization 1995 (%) | 48.8 (17.00) | 37.3 (17.78) | -2.01** | 32 (13.83) | -2.67*** |
| Professionalism 2000 (%) | 14.8 (5.19) | 13.9 (3.85) | -0.62 | 16.2 (3.27) | 0.79 |
| Years | 2.2 (3.25) | 8.9 (5.06) | 4.46*** | 9.9 (2.80) | 5.78*** |
| Court orders 95 | 1.5 (2.50) | 8.4 (14.46) | 2.09** | 2.6 (4.52) | 0.86 |
| State prisoners 2003 | 13.8 (15.8) | 45 (44.5) | 2.95*** | 11.9 (9.5) | -0.36 |
| Number of states | 20 | 20 | | 10 | |

Note: States are grouped according to their magnitude of SPP in 2003. The t-test is made by comparing non-SPP states with modest and significant SPP states. Northeast is included.

* Significant at .1 level. ** Significant at .05 level. *** Significant at .01 level.

## 4.4. DATA STRUCTURE

The data used in this study are secondary and cross-sectional data, with three important structural characteristics:

**Table 4.5. Average SPP levels across two groups of states**

|  | Average value of IVs of Group 1 | Average SPP level of Group 1 (%) | Average value of IVs of Group 2 | Average SPP level of Group 2 (%) | t-value |
|---|---|---|---|---|---|
| Overcrowding 95(%) | 97 (3.68) | 8.6 (11.33) | 116 (17.04) | 5.3 (9.47) | -1.12 |
| PCE 96 (%) | 2.6 (0.61) | 6 (10.27) | 4.6 (0.99) | 7.9 (10.79) | 0.64 |
| TSL 95 | 0 (0) | 5 (10.2) | 1 (0) | 8.76 (10.59) | 1.28 |
| PIOC 96 ($1000) | 16.1 (3.46) | 7.5 (9.24) | 27.9 (4.75) | 6.4 (11.74) | -0.37 |
| State policy liberalism | -0.86 (0.4) | 10.98 (12.06) | 0.81 (0.55) | 2.93 (6.67) | -2.92*** |
| Northeast | 0 (0) | 8.18 (11.12) | 1 (0) | 1.38 (3.17) | -3.35*** |
| Midwest | 0 (0) | 8.7 (11.41) | 1 (0) | 1.43 (2.57) | -3.65*** |
| South | 0 (0) | 6.82 (11.62) | 1 (0) | 7.24 (7.81) | 0.15 |
| West | 0 (0) | 3.93 (6.18) | 1 (0) | 15.55 (14.9) | 2.72*** |
| Unionization 1995 (%) | 25.6 (6.83) | 9.4 (11.13) | 56 (10.73) | 4.6 (9.38) | -1.65* |
| Professionalism 2000 (%) | 11.4 (3.1) | 5.7 (8.08) | 18 (2.4) | 8.19 (12.46) | 0.84 |
| Years | 2.08 (2.27) | 0.94 (2.3) | 10.76 (3.5) | 12.96 (11.97) | 4.93*** |
| Court orders 95 | 0.16 (0.37) | 4.87 (8.64) | 8.76(12.7) | 9.03 (11.83) | 1.42 |
| State prisoners 2003 | 6.73 (4.42) | 7.58 (13.24) | 45.1 (39) | 6.32 (6.9) | -0.42 |

Note: The states are grouped according to the values of every IV. For continuous variables, every group has 25 states. Group 1 has the 25 states with the lowest values of the IVs. For dummy variables, the groups are naturally divided. As a result, for different IVs, the two groups are different. The northeast region is also included. The figures in the parentheses are standard deviations. The t-test is made by comparing the means of SPP levels for the two groups of states.
* Significant at .1 level. ** Significant at .05 level. *** Significant at .01 level.

The dependent variable is censored. A large proportion of censored data has a limiting value, usually zero, which constitutes the bound of the data's continuous distribution. When there is a heavy concentration on the bound, the distribution of censored data is a mixture of discrete and continuous distribution. The dependent variable of this research is the 2003 SPP levels of the 50 US states.[18] Because the percentage of prisoners outsourced is used, the lowest level is 0. There is no negative value since it is not possible for state prisons to admit prisoners who are under the legal authority of private criminal justice systems, at least not currently. This dependent variable shows a high right-skewness: 20 states (40% of the observations) have a bound value of 0 while 30 SPP states have SPP levels between 0.2% and 44.2%. Section 4.5 will briefly discuss the appropriate statistical method for a censored dependent variable.

The temporal effects exist and are incorporated into the data structure. There are two relevant concerns. One is that the pattern of the distribution of SPP levels among the states came into being in 1999. Figure 4.4 shows that the five years between 1999 and 2003 share almost identical patterns for the distribution of SPP levels, except in 2000 when Alabama and Delaware had a temporary high reliance on SPP. After 1999, the nationwide growth of SPP slowed down and settled into a period of marginal fine-tuning. This suggests that the distribution of SPP levels among these years is determined by similar factors.[19] This is not surprising because major developments in SPP had taken place before 1999 and especially during the 1995-1999 period.[20]

Another temporal concern is that it is time-consuming for governments to operationalize SPP decisions. It takes an extended period of time for an SPP proposal to satisfy many procedural requirements, survive political opposition, and become a public decision. It also takes a considerable amount of time to write requests for proposal (RFP), to negotiate contracts, to procure land, and to design and build correctional facilities.[21] Additional time is needed for the facilities to become fully operational due to staff recruitment, training and prisoner admission, etc. As a result, the proportion of prisoners currently outsourced is explained by decisional contexts that existed three or more years ago. Combined with the first temporal concern, the decisional situation in the

---

[18] DC is not included due to its takeover by BOP in 2001.

[19] Table 5.3 shows that the results of Tobit regressions across 1999-2003 are similar and consistent.

[20] During 1995-1999, the number of private state prisons increased by 140% from 98 to 238 and the number of state prisoners outsourced increased by 337% from 15,408 to 67,380. During the same period, 17 states outsourced prisoners for the first time.

[21] Private firms can complete the design and construction of facilities in 12 to 24 months, compared to government's 36-48 months (CCA Web: http://www.correctionscorp .com/4main.html#value).

mid 1990s may determine the distribution of SPP levels across states during and after 1999. Based on the available data, the data of the independent variables (IVs) are mainly collected from the year 1995 or 1996.

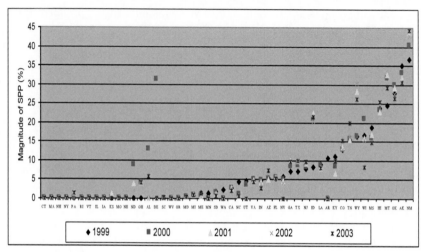

Sources: BJS (2000a, 2001, 2002a, 2003b, 2004a).

Figure 4.4. SPP levels across states, 1999-2003.

Finally, due to the existence of private state prisons in the mid 1990s, the information about state prison systems includes that of private prisons. This is acceptable since private prisons are one part of state prison systems and the pressures faced by private prisons will be naturally conveyed to state governments, such as overcrowding and court orders. Since the mid 1990s SPP levels were in general very low, the data represent mainly public prison systems.

## 4.5. TOBIT ANALYSIS: THE REDUCED AND THE COMPLETE MODELS

The descriptive statistical information of the data in Section 4.3 is limited in that it does not control the multivariate influences among the explanatory variables. Nor does it consider the skewness of the dependent variable. While a multivariate regression can control the multivariate influences, it must take into consideration the structure of the dependent variable.

The dependent variable, the SPP level, is censored and concentrated on zero. The skewness of y and the nonlinear relation between y and the IVs seriously violate the assumptions of OLS regression: the linear relationship between y and X and the homoscedasticity of y.[22] The OLS model may predict y values out of the bound that can not be interpreted. Meanwhile, the Logit model and Probit models, by converting y into a binary variable, simplify the censored data as dichotomous data, lose the substantive information of y, and can not reflect the differences between SPP states.

The Tobit model was invented by Tobin (1958) to treat censored data. It creates an underlying index to represent the latent variable whose value is only observable when it is positive, and keeps all the original information of the dependent variable. As a result, the substantive information of the positive observations is kept while the bound observations are indexed in a way to reflect the unobservable information of these observations. To use the Tobit model, the IVs should influence simultaneously the likelihood of the bound observations to take a non-bound value and the magnitude of the non-bound observations (McDonald and Moffitt, 1980). The Tobit model is a hybrid of the Probit model and the linear regression model. It overcomes the inefficiency of the Probit model due to its loss of information and it also avoids violating the assumptions of the linear model. Use of the Tobit model in social science research is increasing. For example, it is used to research the relationship between court toughness and the attributes of criminals and their communities (Helms and Jacobs, 2002), the relationship between government funding and on-the-job training (Gunderson, 1974), and the relationship between political campaign contributions and access to politicians (Langbein, 1986).

The stochastic Tobit model is: $y = f(X) = Max(0, Xb + U)$. $Xb + U$ is a latent linear index with X denoting the independent variables and b being the Tobit coefficients. The error term U is assumed to be independently and normally distributed. The dependent variable, the SPP level, will have a value of zero if the index is not larger than 0. (ref. Appendix F for the mathematical description of Tobit analysis).

In the research, the independent variables have several components: instrumental factors, political factors, other factors, and the control variable (ref. Table 4.3). As explained at the end of Section 1.2, I intend to use two models: the reduced and the complete, to examine the separate effects of

---

[22] Homoscedasticity refers to the situation that the conditional distribution of y has constant standard deviation throughout the range of the explanatory variables.

instrumental factors and the combined effects of instrumental and political factors. The two models are specified as follows:

Reduce model: $y = f(Xi, Xo, Xc)$
Complete model: $y = f(Xi, Xp, Xo, Xc)$

Xi, Xp, Xo and Xc denote respectively instrumental factors, political factors, other factors, and the control variable. While I assume the comprehensive decision rationality in the SPP decision, omission of political factors may lead to biased results of the reduce model. The level of such biasness may suggest the necessity of considering both political and instrumental factors in analyzing SPP.

For the mathematical description of Tobit analysis, please refer to Appendix F.


## 4.6. RECAPITULATION

In Chapter 4, I discuss the research design to examine the variation in the magnitude of SPP among states in 2003. The data are censored and the Tobit model is identified as the appropriate statistical method. The descriptive statistics shows that political factors, including state policy liberalism, regional effect, and unionization, have consistent effect on the magnitude of SPP, while instrumental factors have inconsistent effects or even effects contrary to the theoretical expectation. The years variable also has very consistent positive effect on the cumulation of SPP. The next chapter will use multivariate Tobit regression to examine the effects of these variables.

# Chapter 5

# RESULTS

## INTRODUCTION

In this chapter, I analyze the results of the Tobit models. After comparing the results of the reduced and the complete models, I will discuss the independent variables (IVs) in the complete model. Further, the Tobit model will be used to examine the magnitude of state prison privatization (SPP) across the 1999-2003 period. The probabilistic and substantive effects of the explanatory variables on SPP will be analyzed. Different methods will be used to examine the robustness of the data. Finally, Tobit analysis will be used to explain the national trend of SPP.

## 5.1. THE RESULTS OF THE TOBIT MODELS

According to my hypothesis that SPP decisions are fundamentally driven by political factors yet instrumental factors have the most direct effect on the magnitude of SPP, the two Tobit models are designed in Section 4.5 to examine the relative capacity of instrumental and political factors in explaining the magnitude of SPP in states. Influences of individual variables are examined according to the results of the complete model, and are further examined by extending Tobit analysis to state SPP decisions between 1999 and 2003.

## 5.1.1. Comparison between the Reduced and the Complete Models

Table 5.1 shows the results of the two Tobit models. Overall, the Tobit results exhibit a good fit with theoretical expectations. The results show that instrumental factors can influence SPP decisions, that political factors have important influences and can moderate the effects of instrumental factors, and that other factors may also be important, such as the years variable that reflects the institutionalization effects of SPP.

The reduced model demonstrates that combined with some non-political factors, most instrumental factors (overcrowding, proportion of correctional expenditures [PCE], and per inmate operating cost [PIOC]) have a significant influence and explain a considerable portion of the variation in the SPP magnitude within states, with a Pseudo R-square of 0.42.[1] The whole model has a significant Chi-square value of 32. Most instrumental variables have expected signs, except for PIOC that, not surprisingly, has a negative effect. Without controlling political factors, high correctional cost may, contrary to theory, be a good indicator of states' decreasing enthusiasm for SPP, as discussed in Chapter 2.

The complete model pools the effects of instrumental and political factors and identifies the significant influence of both groups of factors. Major political factors (state policy liberalism and regions) have significant and expected influence. Unexpectedly, unionization shows a small positive but insignificant effect, which is mainly due to the high correlation between unionization and state policy liberalism (ref. Section 5.1.2). This model shows that the effect of political factors are not limited to placing SPP into motion; instead, they can directly influence decisions on contract-making, and thus the magnitude of SPP. The adding of political factors increases the Pseudo R-square by 36% from 0.42 to 0.57. The whole model has a significant Chi-square value of 42. Further, in the complete model, PIOC has a significant and positive effect on SPP. Such a multivariate interaction between PIOC and political factors may suggest that cost efficiency concern may be highly contingent on the political context.

---

[1] Pseudo R-square of Tobit analysis is calculated through maximum likelihood method as an approximation to the R-square of OLS regression.

**Table 5.1. Tobit results of the reduced and the complete models**

| Variable | Reduced model | Complete model |
|---|---|---|
| Overcrowding 95 | 0.24*** (0.044) | 0.36*** (0.056) |
| PCE 96 | 2.02* (1.126) | 1.3 (1.057) |
| TSL 95 | 5.21 (3.425) | 3.12 (3.056) |
| PIOC 96 | -0.22* (0.137) | 0.43*** (0.153) |
| State policy liberalism | | -5.21** (2.502) |
| Midwest | | -1.75 (4.51) |
| South | | 10.19** (4.98) |
| West | | 10.81*** (4.297) |
| Unionization 95 | | 0.01 (0.068) |
| Professionalism 2000 | | 0.22 (0.22) |
| Years | 2.35*** (0.418) | 1.66*** (0.423) |
| Court orders 95 | -0.21 (0.178) | -0.27 (0.173) |
| Prisoners 2003 | -0.18*** (0.06) | -0.08 (0.063) |
| Constant | -38.04*** (6.674) | -69.35*** (10.599) |
| | | |
| Chi-square | 32*** (P<0.001) | 42*** (p<0.001) |
| Pseudo R-square | 0.42 | 0.57 |
| N | 50 | 50 |

Dependent variable: The magnitude of SPP in 2003.
Note: Within the parentheses are standard errors.
* Significant at .1 level; ** Significant at .05 level; *** Significant at .01 level.

Finally, some other factors that can not be simply classified as political or instrumental, can also influence the magnitude of SPP. The years variable has a significant and powerful positive effect on SPP, showing that states' previous practice in SPP may establish a path for future decisions. Such a path may be strengthened over time. Both the number of court orders and the number of state prisoners have negative impact on SPP, yet their influences are not significant.

In the following section, I will discuss each individual factor according to the results of the complete model.

## 5.1.2. A Discussion on the Decision Factors

A Tobit coefficient is not directly meaningful except for its sign and statistical significance.[2] Before I differentiate the Tobit effect as a probability effect on non-SPP states and a substantive effect on SPP states in the next section, I will discuss the Tobit results of the complete model as far as the sign and significance are concerned.

### *Rate of Overcrowding*

Prison overcrowding has a consistently significant and positive influence on SPP. This result corresponds to the common consensus on the importance of overcrowding in the SPP literature and in the survey by McDonald et al. (1998), but is contrary to the consistently insignificant result of prison overcrowding in Nicholson-Crotty's (2004) research.[3] He argues that it might be due to the reduced federal court pressures on overcrowded state prison systems since the mid 1990s. My result suggests that overcrowding may bring about pressure from various actors besides the federal courts. And the most important one should be the law-and-order politicians who care about the sustainability of the operation of the whole criminal justice system, but have less concern on how well prisoners are incarcerated, and do not want "get tough on crime" policies to be constrained by prison overcrowding. The story behind the existence of two public agencies implementing SPP policy in Florida is one excellent example.[4]

### *PCE and TSL*

Proportion of correctional expenditures (PCE) and tax and spending limits legislation (TSL) measure the financial motivations for SPP. Both of them are positive as hypothesized but are insignificant. The positive impact of the overall financial burden on SPP is confirmed, without achieving statistical

---

[2] The Tobit effect has different implications for different states. For non-SPP states, the Tobit effect estimates the effect of IVs on the probability to outsource prisoners; for SPP states, the Tobit effect estimates the effect of IVs on the magnitude of SPP. Thus the substantive meaning of a Tobit coefficient must be further revealed. In Section 5.2, this issue will be discussed.

[3] Nicholson-Cortty does not consider the time-lag effect, as I do in this research. The positive influence of the current overcrowding level on SPP is not instant, rather, such influence often extends into the future. Since he uses the overcrowding and the existence of SPP contracts in same years, his model's specification is likely to reflect the negative influence of existing SPP contracts on the current overcrowding level.

[4] Ref. Footnote 3 of Chapter 4.

significance. A possible explanation for the insignificance regarding PCE may be the existence of a self-selection effect in that a higher percentage of state expenditure on corrections directly reflects the willingness or capacity of the state to spend money on corrections. Those states with low proportions of state money spent on corrections may either have antipathy to the increase of correctional budgets or have less taxing capacity to support it, and may thus be inclined to introduce SPP. This self-selection effect can dilute the influence of PCE.

The positive sign of TSL indicates that it would likely be placing downward pressure on correctional expenditures, thus favoring SPP. Yet, the insignificance of TSL may suggest that politicians can strategically manipulate the implementation of TSL to their own advantage and thus reduce the effectiveness of TSL in limiting correctional expenditures. While TSL sets constraints on the total state budget, such constraints may be structured in a way that favors justice and especially correctional expenditures. Clingermayer and Wood (1995) find weak evidence that TSL may increase state indebtedness and "constitutional debt limitations have no effect upon slowing the growth of state debt" (p.108). Most TSL states introduced TSL before 1995 and their correctional budget increases did not show any indication of slowing down compared to non-TSL states.[5]

## Per Inmate Operating Cost

In the complete model per inmate operating cost (PIOC) has a significant and positive coefficient. High correctional cost does favor SPP. Considering the generally negative effect of PIOC on SPP, as is shown in the descriptive statistics and the reduced model, this result suggests that the correct explanatory power of PIOC may have to be identified while relevant political variables are controlled. In other words, states' attitude toward PIOC may be highly influenced by a self-selection effect: a high PIOC can reflect states' financial capacity of operating expensive prisons or political commitment to rehabilitative goals, thus a weak desire for SPP.

## State Policy Liberalism:

State policy liberalism, as expected, has a significant and negative influence on SPP, showing that a conservative state political environment favors SPP. The importance of the political environment is not exclusively based on its ideological attitude toward the transfer of correction-related

---

[5] Among the 27 TSL states in 2003, only Oregon introduced it after 1995.

expenditures to the private sector, but also on its attitude toward cost efficiency. Although the result of state policy liberalism fits well with theoretical expectations, the data may be somewhat dated since its calculation is based on the period 1974-1985. States may have experienced changes after 1985. As a matter of fact, one policy issue for the calculation of the composite policy liberalism score, *Aid to Families with Dependent Children*, was nationally ended during my research period. Nonetheless, these data should be valid since general political culture is likely to be stable at least for a decade. The very high correlation between state policy liberalism and the unionization level in 1995 may be a good demonstration of the stableness of the former over time.

### South and West

The result of the complete model shows that being a southern or western state will significantly strengthen the state's inclination to privatize prisons compared to being located in the northeast. The path-dependent effect in social control and the learning and transfer of SPP practices within the same region are important, and these effects are further amplified by the existence of regional SPP leaders.[6] Being a midwestern state does not have statistically significant impact on the magnitude of SPP compared to a northeastern state. The slightly bigger coefficient of the west suggests that western states are a little more aggressive in heavily using SPP than southern states, despite the fact that the south is the national leader in SPP, has the majority of private prisoners, and has the largest prisoner import. This is mainly due to the distribution pattern of SPP levels for these two regions. The SPP levels of western states have a more imbalanced distribution than southern states. There are many extremely large values in western states. In 2003, 6 of the 7 states with SPP levels greater than 20% were located in the west. So although the south has a greater overall regional SPP level (8.2%) than that of the west (6%), the average SPP level of southern states (7.2%) is smaller than that of western states (15.6%). This does not indicate a serious distortion of the true information. For example, despite its largest private prison system that dwarfs any other western state, Texas only privatized 9.9 percent of its prisoners in 2003 and operated a public prison system whose scale was only next to

---

[6] A spatial analysis has been done, but does not identify the existence of spatial autocorrelation among the bordering states. This may suggest that the path-dependent effect and policy transfer effect are not mainly based on geographical contiguity, but on the cultural contiguity in the style of social control. As such, it is more valid to consider the culturally defined regions rather than the geographically defined bordering states.

California's in 2003. Texas did have a comparatively lower reliance on the private sector compared to many western states.

## *Unionization*

Unionization has a very small, positive, and insignificant coefficient, which conflicts with the hypothesized negative influence of unions on SPP. While public unions and the private prison industry are both advocates of the prison industrial complex, their competing interests make it a zero-sum game in the competition for correctional funds. Unions struggle to shape the use of correctional money and see privatization as a serious threat to their bargaining power, thus to the compensation and job security of their members. There are numerous examples where unions have successfully stopped SPP intentions through intense political opposition (Parenti, 2003). Consequently, it is highly suspected that the insignificant result is derived from the existence of a high collinearity. The data show a strong correlation of 0.81 between state policy liberalism and unionization. In fact, a high correlation between state political culture and the level of unionization is very likely in as much as the political environment determines the feasibility of unionization and conditions the functioning of unions, thus making the level of unionization a byproduct of it. Statistically, they appear as virtual surrogate variables to one another. Table 5.2 shows the Tobit results when either unionization or state policy liberalism is excluded from the complete model. In either case, they are negative and significant, and the absence of either one does not bring about a serious impact on other IVs and on the whole model, especially when unionization is excluded. This result indicates that unionization has a significant influence on SPP. Unions are active in opposing SPP, and their actions are most effective in liberal states. Nicholson-Crotty's (2004, p.53) statement that "public employee unions simply do not wield power over the privatization process" may not be entirely, even mostly, correct.

## *Professionalism*

Considering the deprofessionalization effect of conservative social control on corrections, I test the influence of correctional professionals on SPP. The percentage of professionals in the correctional staff does not exhibit a significant influence and fails to prove the importance of correctional professionals in pushing forward SPP. The result indicates that the proxy is likely invalid in representing the influence of professionalism or that the correctional professionals are not a serious force in influencing SPP.

*Years*

The years variable is significant in having a positive influence on SPP. It reflects the institutionalization of SPP practices that embed SPP into correctional systems through various channels (ref. Section 4.2.3). These various institutionalization forces can be represented by the elapse of time in states' involvement in SPP. The significance of the temporal effect indicates that SPP practices are incremental, in that previous SPP practices strengthen existing paths and invite further privatization. Longer duration of SPP practices tend to increase the dependence of state governments on the private sector, and make the reversion a difficult, if not an impossible, option.

**Table 5.2. Tobit results with/without unionization**

|  | Complete model | Adjusted model | |
|---|---|---|---|
|  |  | Without liberalism | Without unionization |
| Overcrowding 95 | 0.36*** (0.056) | 0.33*** (0.053) | 0.36*** (0.056) |
| PCE 96 | 1.3 (1.057) | 0.66 (1.041) | 1.28 (1.041) |
| TSL 95 | 3.12 (3.056) | 3.02 (3.489) | 3.15 (3.485) |
| PIOC 96 | 0.43*** (0.153) | 0.24* (0.143) | 0.44*** (0.153) |
| **State policy liberalism** | **-5.21** (2.502)** |  | **-5.12** (2.327)** |
| Midwest | -1.75 (4.51) | -3.06 (4.446) | -1.85 (4.602) |
| South | 10.19** (4.98) | 8.39** (4.341) | 10.04** (5.086) |
| West | 10.81*** (4.297) | 10.37*** (4.25) | 10.72** (4.435) |
| **Unionization 95** | **0.01 (0.068)** | **-0.18*** (0.068)** |  |
| Professionalism 2000 | 0.22 (0.22) | 0.21 (0.225) | 0.22 (0.228) |
| Years | 1.66*** (0.423) | 1.71*** (0.416) | 1.65*** (0.42) |
| Court orders 95 | -0.27 (0.173) | -0.21 (0.174) | -0.28 (0.178) |
| Prisoners in 2003 | -0.08 (0.063) | -0.09* (0.055) | -0.08 (0.063) |
| Constant | -69.35*** (10.599) | -50.36*** (8.2) | -68.82*** (10.445) |
|  |  |  |  |
| Chi-square | 42*** (p<0.001) | 40***(p<0.001) | 42*** (p<0.001) |
| Pseudo R-square | 0.57 | 0.57 | 0.57 |
| N | 50 | 50 | 50 |

Dependent variable: The magnitude of SPP in 2003
Note: Within the parentheses are standard errors
* Significant at .1 level; ** Significant at .05 level; *** Significant at .01 level.

## Court Orders

Federal court orders show no effect on SPP. There are several possible explanations. One is the credibility of the data in reflecting court pressure. The data do not reflect court orders imposed on entire state correctional systems. In 2003, those states whose State Department of Corrections (SDOCs) were ever under court order to limit overcrowding during 1978-1985 (Levitt, 1996), had an average SPP rate of 13.1%, almost twice the average level of SPP nationwide. My data may not exactly measure the pressure imposed on state decision-makers. It is also true that since the mid 1990s, represented by the passage of the *1996 Prisoner Litigation Reform Act*, court pressure waned as courts retreat from decades of a "hands-on" approach in dealing with prison administration. In fact, it is not rare in the history of prison litigation that correctional officials failed to demonstrate compliance or even "openly obstructed compliance and disobeyed court orders" (Belbot, 2004, p.307; Crouch and Marquart, 1989; Yackle, 1989). Finally, while court orders leave discretion to prison administrators regarding the ways to comply with court orders, SPP may not be the first choice. The long life cycle of court orders shows that federal courts are not proactive in issuing and enforcing their orders.[7] The mild pressure from courts may not compel SDOCs into SPP, but give them time to relieve overcrowding through various administrative means. In the long run, court orders may help to prevent overcrowding, thus preclude the necessity of SPP.

## 5.1.3. Tobit Results across 1999-2003 Period

Cross-sectional data may not be stable over time. To avoid biased results due to the selection of the research year, and to examine my argument that decision situations in the mid 1990s determine the distribution of SPP across states since 1999, I use the Tobit model to analyze the magnitude of SPP during 1999-2003. The data for the 5 Tobit regressions will mostly remain unchanged, except for the dependent variable (the magnitude of SPP), the years variable, and the number of prisoners variable. These three variables have yearly data. Table 5.3 shows the results of 5 Tobit regressions for these 5

---

[7] According to Levitt (1996), the life cycle of a court order includes prefiling, filed, preliminary decision, final decision, further action, and release, often spanning two decades. There is a long time between prefiling and the issuing of a court order.

years. Due to the high collinearity between state policy liberalism and unionization, the unionization variable is removed from these regressions.

**Table 5.3. Tobit results of the magnitude of SPP across 1999-2003**

|  | 2003 | 2002 | 2001 | 2000 | 1999 |
|---|---|---|---|---|---|
| Overcrowding 95 | 0.36*** (0.056) | 0.35*** (0.054) | 0.35*** (0.056) | 0.31*** (0.051) | 0.29*** (0.045) |
| PCE 96 | 1.28 (1.041) | 1.69 (1.069) | 2.52** (1.161) | 1.52 (1.139) | 1.41 (0.887) |
| TSL 95 | 3.15 (3.485) | 3.34 (3.546) | 3.06 (3.696) | 6.55* (3.939) | 5.47* (3.191) |
| PIOC 96 | 0.44*** (0.153) | 0.31** (0.14) | 0.26* (0.146) | 0.32** (0.149) | 0.91*** (0.171) |
| State policy liberalism | -5.12** (2.327) | -4.11* (2.272) | -4.03* (2.428) | -2.39 (2.32) | -6.15*** (2.016) |
| Midwest | -1.85 (4.602) | 0.65 (4.221) | 1.42 (4.686) | 7.34 (4.854) | 5.28 (3.952) |
| South | 10.04** (5.086) | 7.58 (4.954) | 5.48 (5.131) | 20.14*** (5.47) | 16.84*** (4.64) |
| West | 10.72** (4.435) | 10.61** (4.603) | 10.13** (4.939) | 17.94*** (5.712) | 15.17*** (4.738) |
| Professionalism 2000 | 0.22 (0.228) | 0.26 (0.228) | 0.16 (0.239) | -0.17 (0.229) | -0.05 (0.192) |
| Years (2003-1999) | 1.65*** (0.42) | 4.09*** (1) | 2.04*** (0.528) | 1.07** (0.532) | 1.17*** (0.453) |
| Court orders 95 | -0.28 (0.178) | -0.23 (0.177) | -0.29 (0.198) | -0.37* (0.194) | -0.34** (0.156) |
| Prisoners (2003-1999) | -0.08 (0.063) | -0.1* (0.058) | -0.12* (0.064) | -0.11* (0.068) | -0.05 (0.048) |
| Constant | -68.82*** (10.445) | -66.09*** (9.689) | -65.16*** (9.909) | -56.91*** (8.886) | -67.7*** (9.53) |
| Log likelihood | -118 | -121 | -125 | -132 | -119 |
| Pseudo R-square | 0.57 | 0.52 | 0.44 | 0.37 | 0.46 |
| N | 50 | 50 | 50 | 50 | 50 |

Dependent variable: The magnitude of SPP in 1999-2003

Note: Only y, years, and prisoners have different data across 1999-2003. Within the
    parentheses are standard errors.

* Significant at .1 level; ** Significant at .05 level; *** Significant at .01 level.

Table 5.3 shows that the regression results are consistent across the 1999-2003 period despite some slight fluctuations. The results discussed in Sections 5.1.1 regarding the overall model fitness and in Section 5.1.2 regarding the properties of individual IVs are confirmed. The Tobit results are not sensitive to the choice of any of these 5 years for research. Overcrowding, per inmate operating cost, state policy liberalism, regions (south and west), and years remain significant with expected directions of influence in most of the regressions. Only the midwest region variable and professionalism variable are insignificant throughout the regressions. Proportion of correctional expenditures, tax and spending limits, and court orders have significant results in one or two years, indicating that their influence may not be negligible. The control variable, the number of state prisoners, has a weakly significant result (at 0.1 level) in three years, showing that a large prison population may be a restriction on the magnitude of SPP.

## 5.1.4. A comparison between New York and New Mexico

A straightforward way to observe the fundamental importance of politics in SPP is to directly compare individual states that are similar in instrumental aspects but different in politics. Table 5.4 takes New Mexico and New York for a comparison. Prison systems of these two states faced similar instrumental situations in the mid 1990s. Only overcrowding rate of New York was slightly higher. Meanwhile, although New York has a per capita income about 50% higher than New Mexico, its per resident correctional burden is also about 50% higher than New Mexico. From the instrumental perspective, these two states should not be very different in terms of their demand functions of SPP, and New York may be a little more likely to use prison privatization since its prisoner population is about 10 times that of New Mexico. The fact is, until 2003, New Mexico had been outsourcing prisoner for 15 years and had the highest SPP level in the US, while New York had never used an SPP contract.

Such difference can only be explained by politics. New Mexico is a western conservative state. Although it does not have the right to work law, its unionization level is low. It shares a punitive politics of law and order with its neighbor, Texas, which has the nation's largest private prison system. Previous Republican Governor Gary Johnson was a strong SPP advocate with an intention to completely privatize the prison system. His penal policy called for prisoners to serve "every stinking minute" of their sentences and for the deprivation of even minimal comforts in the newest state prisons (Greene,

2000). "No electrical outlets were installed in the cells to allow operation of televisions or radios" (ibid).

**Table 5.4. A comparison between New York and New Mexico regarding SPP**

|         | SPP 2003 (%) | Overcrowding 95 (%) | PCE 96 (%) | TSL 95 | PIOC 96 ($1,000) |
|---------|--------------|---------------------|------------|--------|------------------|
| New York | 0 | 102 | 3.72 | 0 | 28.4 |
| New Mexico | 44.2 | 96 | 3.67 | 0 | 29.5 |
|         | State policy liberalism | Unionization 95 (%) | Region | | |
| New York | 2.12 | 73.6 | Northeast | | |
| New Mexico | -0.99 | 25.2 | West | | |

Comparatively, New York is a northeastern and traditionally liberal state. The unionization level in New York's public sector is one of the highest in the country. This political environment makes it hard to initiate the SPP policy, and in fact, as a response to the national SPP fashion, New York enacted law in 2000 to ban the privatization of correctional facilities, under the pressures from labor unions and other groups.

## 5.2. PROBABILISTIC AND SUBSTANTIVE EFFECTS OF THE EXPLANATORY VARIABLES

The effects of the explanatory variables on SPP are contingent on the SPP status for every state. For the 20 non-SPP states, these factors exert influence by changing their probability to outsource prisoners; for the other 30 SPP states, they change their desired magnitude of SPP.[8] In this section, I will

---

[8] Some scholars further decompose the Tobit effect. Appendix F shows that a change in the expected SPP level for SPP states due to a change in independent variables can always be attributed to two parts: the probability effect (Part II) and the substantive effect (Part I).

substantiate the influence of the explanatory factors on these two different groups of states.

The Tobit model is nonlinear and the Tobit effect is contingent on the very point of observation. In this discussion, I will choose the probability of outsourcing prisoners, namely F(z), at a value of 0.6 as the reference point.[9] For non-SPP states, the change in the probability, $\Delta$F(z), is calculated by formula f(z)b/s. For SPP states, the change in the expected level of SPP, $\Delta$Ey, is calculated by bF(z). b is the Tobit coefficient of the explanatory variable, s is the model's standard error, f(z) is the standard normal density function (ref. Appendix F).

Table 5.5 makes the results of the Tobit regression interpretable in a straightforward manner. The regression does not include unionization, so the decomposition is based on the results in Table 5.2. Table 5.5 shows, for example, that if the overcrowding rate increases by 1 percent, an SPP state is expected to increase its SPP level by 0.21 percent, and a non-SPP state is expected to increase its chance to outsource prisoners by 1.34 percent, given a F(z) value of 0.6. Further, information in Table 5.5 helps to disclose how powerful the influence of these IVs may be. Take the influence of the IVs on the expected level of SPP as an example. Given a reference point with F(z) equal to 0.6, to maintain the same SPP level, a change from northeast to south or west needs a decrease in overcrowding by 29 or 32 percent, an increase in state policy liberalism by one unit needs an increase in overcrowding by 15 percent, and an increase of per inmate operating cost by 10,000 dollars needs a decrease of overcrowding by 10 percent, given other factors. This does not necessarily mean that political factors are more powerful than instrumental factors, since the ranges of instrumental factors are larger.

The differentiation of the Tobit effects can be further used to examine the prediction error of the 50 states. For the probability of outsourcing prisoners, 17 of the 20 non-SPP states are correctly predicted to have no prisoners outsourced, and to a similar extent, 24 of the 30 SPP states are correctly predicted to outsource prisoners in 2003. For non-SPP states, the 3 wrong predictions (Arkansas, Nevada, and Utah) are all southern or western states, while 3 (Michigan, Maine, and Wisconsin) of the 6 wrong predictions for SPP

---

Appendix G shows a decomposition of the Tobit effect along this way. Such decomposition can be explained in a meaningful way only for SPP states. This research will not discuss this.

[9] This figure is the percentage of SPP states in the 50 states in 2003. Selection of 0.6 as a reference point reflects roughly the average probability for a state to outsource prisoners in 2003.

states are northeast or midwest states. This may indicate the importance of
political factors for the Tobit model to make predictions on the probability of
privatization. For the SPP magnitude of the 30 SPP states, an examination of
the residues shows that most large residues exist for the western states. The
average of the absolute value of the residues of 13 southern SPP states is 4.3%,
in contrast to the 9.6% of the 9 western SPP states, showing that the Tobit
model works best in predicting the magnitude of southern SPP states that in
general had modest levels of SPP in 2003.

Table 5.6 takes an SPP state, Ohio, as an example to show the nonlinearity
of the Tobit effect. I measure the effect of the change of years on the expected
level of SPP, given all other factors. In 2003, it had been 4 years since Ohio
first outsourced prisoners in 2000. Table 5.6 shows that when this duration is
extended up to 18 years, the marginal increase of Ey changes from 1.42
percent to 1.65 percent. The marginal increase of the probability to outsource
changes from 3.63 percent to 0.04 percent.

**Table 5.5. Decomposition of the Tobit effects, given F(z)=0.6**

|  | Tobit coefficient | Unit of $\Delta X$ | $\Delta F(z)$ (%) | $\Delta Ey$ (%) |
|---|---|---|---|---|
| Overcrowding 95 | 0.36 | 1 percent | 1.34 | 0.21 |
| PCE 96 | 1.28 | 1 percent | 4.81 | 0.77 |
| TSL 95 | 3.15 | 0 to 1 | 11.82 | 1.89 |
| PIOC 96 | 0.44 | $1000 | 1.64 | 0.26 |
| State policy liberalism | -5.12 | 1 | -19.17 | -3.07 |
| Midwest | -1.85 | 0 to 1 | -6.94 | -1.11 |
| South | 10.04 | 0 to 1 | 37.59 | 6.02 |
| West | 10.72 | 0 to 1 | 40.16 | 6.44 |
| Professionalism 2000 | 0.22 | 1 percent | 0.83 | 0.13 |
| Years | 1.65 | 1 year | 6.20 | 0.99 |
| Court orders 95 | -0.28 | 1 order | -1.04 | -0.17 |
| Prisoners in 2003 | -0.08 | 1000 inmates | -0.29 | -0.05 |

**Table 5.6. The Tobit effect of the variable years on SPP for Ohio, given its 1995 situations**

| Years | Ey | F(z) | ΔEy | ΔF(z) |
|-------|-------|-------|-------|-------|
| 4 | 11.04 | 83.77 | | |
| 5 | 12.46 | 87.40 | 1.42 | 3.63 |
| 6 | 13.93 | 90.42 | 1.47 | 3.02 |
| 7 | 15.45 | 92.88 | 1.52 | 2.45 |
| 8 | 17.00 | 94.81 | 1.55 | 1.94 |
| 9 | 18.58 | 96.31 | 1.58 | 1.49 |
| 10 | 20.19 | 97.43 | 1.60 | 1.12 |
| 11 | 21.81 | 98.25 | 1.62 | 0.82 |
| 12 | 23.44 | 98.84 | 1.63 | 0.59 |
| 13 | 25.08 | 99.24 | 1.64 | 0.41 |
| 14 | 26.72 | 99.52 | 1.64 | 0.28 |
| 15 | 28.37 | 99.70 | 1.65 | 0.18 |
| 16 | 30.02 | 99.82 | 1.65 | 0.12 |
| 17 | 31.67 | 99.89 | 1.65 | 0.07 |
| 18 | 33.33 | 99.94 | 1.65 | 0.04 |
| Total | | | 22.29 | 16.17 |

It is worth noticing that the above calculation of the incremental impacts of IVs on SPP assumes the flexibility of states in fine-tuning their magnitude of SPP, which may not be realistic. The feasibility of states to bring about changes is contingent on many other factors, such as market situations and contractual relationships. For example, states may feel that it is relatively easy to procure prison cells in the market, but relatively difficult to stop sending prisoners to private contractors due to contractual obligations. Another important fact is that this empirical research is based on a scenario of a continuous growth of state prisoner populations. When the number of state prisoners begins to decrease, the effect of the explanatory variables may be different. For example, when the prisoner population decreases, the reduction of overcrowding may not decrease the SPP level. Rather, the SPP level might increase due to the stickiness of SPP contracts.

# 5.3. Comparison between Tobit, Logistic, GLM, and OLS Models[10]

In Section 5.1, I used the Tobit model to analyze the data across 1999 and 2003 and found that the results are not sensitive to the year of research. In this section, I use different models to examine the 2003 data, with a purpose to test the robustness of the data and check the pros and cons of using the Tobit model.

Table 5.7 shows the results of Tobit, Logistic, Generalized Linear Models (GLM) and OLS on the same 2003 data (ref. Appendix H, I, and J). Unionization is excluded due to its high collinearity with state policy liberalism. Table 5.7 shows that in general these models have consistent results, especially for Tobit, GLM, and OLS due to their use of the original SPP data as the dependent variable.

## 5.3.1. Tobit vs. Logistic

Logistic regression transforms the dependent variable to a dummy variable and thus changes the research focus to the existence of prisoner outsourcing or not. Using the same IVs, the Logistic model has similar model fitness and explanatory power as the Tobit model. It has a Chi-square value of 43.6, indicating the significance of the model at the 0.001 level. Its Cox and Snell R-square has a value of 0.58,[11] almost identical to the Pseudo R-square of the Tobit model. The predictive efficiency for the Logistic model is 0.88, a little higher than the 0.8 of the Tobit model.[12] Despite the seemingly better fit of the Logistic model, I have not used it for two reasons. One is that the Logistic model fails to capture the difference in the magnitude of SPP, thus it can not address my research question. Another reason is that the Logistic model fails to correctly reflect the influences of the IVs. For tax and spending limits and western region, their signs are contrary to those of the other three

---

[10] GLM is the acronym for Generalized Linear Models. Tobit, logistic, and OLS are all GLM models. In this research, GLM specifically refers to the method used to process fractional response data (Papke and Wooldridge, 1996).

[11] Cox and Snell's R-Square is an attempt to imitate the interpretation of multiple R-square scores based on the likelihood, but its maximum can be less than 1 and hard to interpret. Nagelkerke R-Square DIVIDES COX AND SNELL'S R-SQUARE BY ITS MAXIMUM, MAKING ITSELF A MEASURE RANGING FROM 0 TO 1. THE SPSS OUTPUT RETURNS A VALUE OF 0.787 FOR Nagelkerke R-square.

[12] Predictive efficiency refers to the percentage of observations for which the statistical model rightly predicts whether the states outsourced prisoners or not.

models. This makes the fit of the Logistic model not as reliable. It is suspected that the specification of the Tobit model, with a purpose to reflect the subtle differences in the magnitude of SPP, creates much redundancy in the Logistic model.

## 5.3.2. Tobit vs. GLM

Using quasi-likelihood method, Generalized Linear Models (GLM) can deal with fractional response variables as an alternative to "linear models that use either y or the log-odds ration of y as the dependent variable" (Papke and Wooldridge, 1996, p.632).

**Table 5.7. Results of Tobit, Logistic, GLM and OLS models on the 2003 SPP level**

| Variable | Tobit | Logistic | GLM | OLS |
|---|---|---|---|---|
| Overcrowding 95 | 0.36*** (0.056) | 0.129* (0.071) | 0.035*** (0.013) | 0.155* (0.093) |
| PCE 96 | 1.28 (1.041) | 1.084 (1.164) | -0.031 (0.165) | -0.385 (1.324) |
| TSL 95 | 3.15 (3.485) | -1.294 (1.887) | 0.2238 (0.348) | 2.793 (2.808) |
| PIOC 96 | 0.44*** (0.153) | 0.070 (0.132) | 0.014 (0.046) | 0.229 (0.29) |
| State policy liberalism | -5.12** (2.327) | -1.123 (1.146) | -0.518* (0.276) | -2.234 (2.02) |
| Midwest | -1.85 (4.602) | -3.910 (3.105) | -0.716 (1.107) | -2.114 (4.193) |
| South | 10.04** (5.086) | 3.162 (3.029) | 1.058 (0.822) | 5.365 (5.536) |
| West | 10.72** (4.435) | -3.120 (3.316) | 1.388* (0.817) | 7.715* (4.437) |
| Professionalism 2000 | 0.22 (0.228) | 0.244 (0.217) | 0.054 (0.043) | 0.286 (0.294) |
| Years | 1.65*** (0.42) | 0.915** (0.471) | 0.154*** (0.04) | 0.910*** (0.307) |
| Court orders 95 | -0.28 (0.178) | 0.067 (0.188) | -0.023 (0.02) | -0.201 (0.155) |
| Prisoners in 2003 | -0.08 (0.063) | 0.079 (0.057) | -0.007 (0.006) | -0.056 (0.054) |
| Constant | -68.82*** (10.445) | -26.388** (13.21) | -9.695*** (1.799) | 25.74* (15.189) |
| Pseudo R-square | 0.57 | 0.58 | | .39 (R² adjusted) |
| N | 50 | 50 | 50 | 50 |

Dependent variable: The magnitude of SPP in 2003.
Note: For Logistic model, Pseudo R-square refers to Cox & Snell R-square. Within the parentheses are standard errors.
* Significant at .1 level; ** Significant at .05 level; *** Significant at .01 level.

Under the GLM (with family [binomial], link [logit], and robust) model, the asymptotic analysis ensures that the predicted values of y will not go beyond the bound of 0 or 1, thus there is no need to adjust the extreme values of 0 and/or 1.[13] Table 5.7 shows that the GLM and Tobit results are very similar. All significant coefficients in the GLM model are also significant in the Tobit model, with the magnitude of these coefficients expanding by roughly ten times in the Tobit model.

One major difference between the GLM model and the Tobit model is their treatment of the bound value, the 20 zero values. The Tobit model was specially invented to deal with the censored data with a concentration of observations on 0, while the GLM model only treats 0 as extreme values due to sampling errors (McDowell, 2004). This makes the GLM model not so appropriate for the left-censored fractional data used by this research. There is no sampling error in the data, which is the population. For the 20 non-SPP states, 10 of them had a stable SPP value of 0 in history. Yet, the results of the GLM regression show that statistical manipulation that takes the bound(s) of SPP levels into consideration can produce better results than OLS regression.

### 5.3.3. Tobit vs. OLS

OLS regression has similar results to GLM and Tobit regressions. While the use of the OLS model for the SPP data violates the assumptions of OLS regression (ref. Section 4.5), the results nevertheless confirm the patterned results in the GLM and Tobit regressions.

## 5.4. A PREDICTION AND EXPLANATION OF THE NATIONAL TREND OF SPP

The longitudinal change of SPP at the national level is worth further explanation and prediction. Figure 1.2 in Chapter 1 shows that the major achievement of SPP in the US was obtained between 1995-1999. This period saw an increase of outsourced state prisoners by 337%. In contrast, the number of outsourced state prisoners in 2003 was only 9% more than that of 1999. The national level of SPP in 2003 was 5.7%, only 0.2% higher than that of 1999.

---

[13] It is assumed that the conditional variance converges to 0 when y has an expected value of 0 or

While the absolute number of state prisoners in private facilities increased by about 7,000 from 1999 to midyear 2004 (BJS, 2005), there was a trend of stagnation in the national SPP level that lingered between 5.5-6% since 1999.

**Table 5.8. Prediction on the national SPP level in 2008**

|  | Year 1995 | Year 2000 | Change | Expected impact on the level of SPP (%) |
|---|---|---|---|---|
| Overcrowding | 114% | 100% | -14% | -2.98 |
| PCE | 4% (96) | 4% (99) | 0 | 0.00 |
| TSL | 0.52 | 0.54 | 0.02 | 0.04 |
| PIOC | $22515 (96) | $22650 (01) | $135 | 0.04 |
| State policy liberalism | -0.02 | -0.02 | 0 | 0.00 |
| Midwest | 0.24 | 0.24 | 0 | 0.00 |
| South | 0.32 | 0.32 | 0 | 0.00 |
| West | 0.26 | 0.26 | 0 | 0.00 |
| Professionalism | 14.7 (2000) | 14.7 | 0 | 0.00 |
| Years | 6.5 | 9.5 | 3 | 3.80 |
| Court orders | 4.46 | 2.86 | -1.6 | 0.31 |
| Prisoners | 25.94 | 28.64 | 2.7 | -0.14 |
| Decision outputs | Year 2003 | Year 2008 |  |  |
| Expected probability of having an SPP contract | 68.7% | 69.7% | 1% |  |
| Expected level of SPP | 7.1% | 7.32% | 0.22% |  |
| Actual level of SPP | 5.7% | Na | Na |  |
| Total |  |  |  | 1.06 |

Sources: BJS (2000b, 2001, 2003a, 2004b, 2004c), Hirsch and Macpherson (1995, 2000).

Note: 1. Data are national data based on the 50 states, not the average of the state data. 2. The calculation of cell (Year, Year 2000) is based on the assumption that there is no new entry or exit of SPP states after 2003. 3. The number in parenthesis shows the data's year if it is different to its column's default year (1995 or 2000). 4. Projection of state prisoners in 2008 is based on an annual growth a 2% since 2003.

The empirical results of my analysis confirm the hypothesized influence of political and instrumental factors on the magnitude of SPP. It is possible to use these results to tentatively predict the change of SPP at the national level in the near future. A simple way is to treat the nation as a hypothesized state influenced by the same political and instrumental factors. This may not be theoretically problematic since the national SPP decision, regarding its decision-makers, decision environment, and outputs, can be reduced to SPP

1.

decisions made independently by the 50 states. Considering the temporal lag between SPP decision situations and SPP outputs (ref. Section 4.4), the national SPP level in 2003 can be explained by the national situations in 1995. And we may use the national situations in 2000 to predict the national SPP level in 2008. Table 5.8 shows the information on the IVs at the national level around 1995 and around 2000. The necessary condition to make this prediction is that nationally, the state prisoner population continues to increase.

The results show that the national SPP level in 2003 is expected to be 7.1%, 2.4% higher than the real figure, and that the probability of this hypothesized state to maintain at least one active SPP contract is expected to be 68.7%. In 2008, such probability is expected to increase by 1% to be 69.7%, while the SPP level is expected to increase by 0.22% to be 7.32%. This suggests that in the near future, the nation will maintain its current SPP level or may expect a very slight increase. Considering the growth of state prisoner populations, the SPP market will still have a slow growth.

The last column of Table 5.8 breaks down this total effect by showing the adjusted effects of the IVs. These effects show the expected changes in the national SPP level due to the change in every IV, given the national situation of 1995. This calculation is only illustrative since these variables change simultaneously. Considering the nonlinearity of Tobit analysis, it is not surprising that the total for these individual effects is 1.06%, different to the expected 0.22% increase obtained from a holistic calculation. It shows that reduction of overcrowding is the major constraint on the growth of SPP between 2003 and 2008, while the increase of years is the major impetus of SPP.

This decomposition has implications. In the recent developing stage of SPP, political and instrumental factors tend to level off and remain stable. Without serious exogenous shock, growth of SPP lies mainly in the private prison industry's efforts to expand markets and solidify its role in corrections. These efforts are reflected by the temporal effect examined in the data analysis. Yet the private industry's expansion constitutes one source of the reduction of overcrowding, which brings about negative impacts on SPP. Because of this, private prison firms have incentives to be strategically proactive in advocating tougher crime control legislation and in supporting law-and-order politicians. The future of the nation's SPP is highly dependent on the continuous overcrowding of public state prisons. So, whether the US custodial state can proceed to deepen this practice in the future will likely determine the fate of SPP.

This prediction can also be used to explain the stagnation of SPP since 1999. The national overcrowding rate of state prisons increased continuously since 1985 to 1993 from 105% to 118%, then decreased continuously to 100% in 2000. Considering the temporal lag, the development of SPP should have peaked during 1995-1999.

Finally, one exogenous policy change that is not controlled in the analysis is the division of crime control between federal and state governments. In recent years, the federal government has greatly strengthened its role in crime control. Between 1995 and 2003, federal prisoners increased by 81%, compared to 24% of state prisoners. In 2002, Bureau of Prisons (BOP) for the first time surpassed California and Texas to be the nation's largest public correctional agency. While crime rates decrease continuously for more than a decade, BOP's expanding role in crime control constitutes a downward influence on SPP due to its constraint on the increase of state prisoners, thus on states' demand for private custodianship. Yet for the private prison industry, BOP does not constitute a threat. In fact, BOP became a major drive of prison privatization in the past several years. The number of federal prisoners outsourced to private facilities increased by 58% from 15,524 in 2000 to 24,506 in midyear 2004, accounting for a quarter of prisoners in private facilities and 79% of the increase of prisoners outsourced from 2000 to midyear 2004 (BJS, 2005). In 2004, the odds of a federal prisoner to end up in a private facility were 2.4 times that of a state prisoner. Combined with outsourcing practices of local jails, the stagnation of SPP may not represent a stagnation of the whole industry of private corrections, or the so-called prison industrial complex.

## 5.5. LIMITS OF THIS RESEARCH

There are some limits in this research. The empirical results may not be stable over time. I only examine the 1995-2003 period due to its critical importance for the nationwide development of SPP and for the formation of the distributive pattern of SPP levels across states. My data do not consider the behavior of governments when prisoner population decreases. Another problem is the data size. While 50 states is roughly qualified for a Large-N-Comparative study (Blomquist, 1999), such cross-sectional data lead to a relatively small data size that may create sensitivity to the change of individual cases. Information overlap exists. Due to the homogenization effect of the institutional environment (DiMaggio and Powell, 1983), and due to the internal relation between political and instrumental issues, the variables used in my model are, to different degrees, correlated. An examination of the variance inflation factor (VIF) (ref. Appendix E) shows that VIF coefficients are still far from close to 10, a level deemed to be a threshold of serious multicollinearity (Neter et al., 1996) and problematic model specification. [14] Even so, the inability to assume complete independence between IVs leads to at least one surprising result, the attenuated effect of unionization in the complete model, due largely to its high correlation with state policy liberalism. Further, the data also have measurement problems. Some variables are not well operationalized; for example, pressure from the courts. And some potential influencing factors, such as lobbying efforts of the private prison industry, can not be measured. Major political variables, such as state policy liberalism and regional dummy variable, may suffer from indirectness in reflecting the represented concepts. Finally, this research has the one policy area in one country problem. So the results may be context-specific and have limited external validity. It will be helpful to extend the research to other core governmental functions and to other countries to examine what may or may not be generalizable from the SPP case in the US.

## 5.6. RECAPITULATION

I find empirical evidence in this chapter that both political and instrumental factors are important in influencing the magnitude of SPP in ways that are theoretically predicted. Political factors are important not only for their direct impact on SPP, but also for their role in inducing and defining instrumental problems. While instrumental factors have a direct influence on SPP, their relevance is contingent on the political environment. Understanding the mutual relationship between political and instrumental factors, the former as the driving force and context of SPP and the latter as the direct pressure on SPP, is indispensable in understanding the fact that less overcrowded and less expensive state prison systems, not coincidently, have higher levels of SPP.

---

[14] Multicollinearity refers to the intercorrelation among the explanatory variables that creates information overlap and specification problems for the explanatory model. The variance inflation factor represents the multiplicative increase in the variance due to one variable being correlated with other explanatory variables and is used to measure the seriousness of the multicollinearity, with a high value indicating serious multicollinearity.

# Chapter 6

# CONCLUSIONS

## INTRODUCTION

This chapter concludes the research on state prison privatization (SPP) and provides policy implications and research directions.

## 6.1. WHY HAVE STATE GOVERNMENTS PRIVATIZED PRISONS?

This research has researched the causes of SPP in the US by examining the influence of political and instrumental factors on SPP, as a case study of the privatization of core governmental functions. A historical and theoretical analysis suggests that political factors drove the prison crisis and shaped the links between instrumental demands and SPP decisions, while instrumental factors produced the most direct explanation of SPP. The empirical analysis demonstrates that both political and instrumental factors make a difference in influencing the magnitude of privatization.

The theoretical analysis of SPP takes a national and historical view in searching for the driving forces of SPP. From this perspective, SPP was driven by two aspects of the self-adjustment in the US since the 1970s: conservative social control and neoliberal economic restructuring. "Get tough on crime" policies directly created serious prison overcrowding and financial pressure on state governments, and also removed the political and moral barriers toward prison privatization by substituting rehabilitative correctional goals with retributive purposes. Conservative social control fundamentally accounted for the demand function of SPP. Meanwhile, neoliberal economic policies sought retrenchment across public policy areas and mandated the transfer of correction-related economic expenditures to the private sector. Besides this distributive purpose, contracting out was also encouraged by neoliberalism as a way to seek efficiency for cost-sensitive governments. While states often treat SPP as a solution to instrumental dilemmas, the general picture is clear that political changes induced instrumental problems and shaped the resolution of these problems.

The empirical analysis applies this logic of political economy by concretely testing the influences of instrumental and political factors on the magnitude of SPP. Instrumental factors are shown to be important, with overcrowding and per inmate operating cost (PIOC) both having significant positive influences. One common problem for instrumental factors is that they face the problem of politics-based self-selection so as to distort their capacity in independently influencing SPP. Their influence on SPP may not make sense without first controlling the political context. For example, states with high PIOC are often observed to be non-SPP states or have low levels of SPP. Plausibly, high PIOC may reflect the political commitment to the rehabilitative model of corrections, and the ideological antipathy to prison privatization. This may also be true for prison overcrowding, whose seriousness may be politically defined. Liberal states have relatively higher rates of overcrowding, but the living condition of their prisoners may not necessarily be worse than the less overcrowded prisons in many conservative states. As a result, liberal states may face less pressure for early release or emergency release, and less pressure from court orders. At the national level, overcrowding is a critically important dynamic variable capable of influencing the national level of SPP over time. The effect of overcrowding, either on the national SPP level or on the SPP level of individual states, is certainly disproportionately distributed among the 50 states; in other words, the major contribution to this effect is from the more conservative states.

The empirical analysis shows that political factors can directly influence the SPP level and moderate the effect of instrumental factors. Politics is the driving force of SPP. The path-dependent style of social control and the conservative-liberal tendency in states' political environment determined the value acceptability and the instrumental relevance of SPP. Being a western or southern state means a wide exposure to the punitive prison culture and to an intense region-based dynamics of conservative crime control and SPP practice. Consequently, western and southern states have a high political and moral tolerance, and also a practical convenience in using SPP. Meanwhile, a highly conservative state political environment prepares ties between governments and industrial-commercial interests and the readiness to adapt to the new policy fashion of SPP. It turns out that the effects of instrumental factors on SPP are conditioned by the nature of the political environment. The more conservative the political environment is; the more sensitive the influence of the instrumental factors is. The comparison between New York and New Mexico suggests that the instrumental problems of state prison systems can be exaggerated, or made prominent, in conservative political contexts.

The empirical results also show that SPP entrenches itself over time through an institutionalization process. The private prison industry struggles to not only integrate itself into the existing system of corrections, but also cultivate its constituencies in the existing political-economic structure. The reliance of state correctional systems and the local economies on the private prison industry can build a path for its continuous growth. In recent years, while overcrowding in public prisons decreases, the future growth of SPP becomes more dependent on the private prison industry and its constituencies to consolidate and expand markets, induce favorable public policies, and strengthen political support.

Beyond SPP, it is possible that increased participation by the private sector in core governmental areas is fundamentally explained by the political motives of governments to expand these functional areas and, simultaneously, to reduce their role in direct service production and delivery. The ironic coexistence of the expansion and retrenchment themes is reconciled through privatization in the form of service outsourcing. The implicit political compromise between these two political motives requires that government growth in principle should keep from fully relying on government employees. Retrenchment of the government is more realistic when it concentrates on the manner of fulfilling public responsibilities rather than the scope of governments. Extended privatization, as the major form of privatizing core functions, effectively connects the two themes. As a result, it becomes politically feasible to gradually reconceptualize core functions of the government and push forward their privatization.

## 6.2. POLICY IMPLICATIONS AND FUTURE RESEARCH DIRECTIONS

This research speaks to real policy issues regarding SPP, and also to future research directions that may overcome the limitations of this research.

My research shows that governments have a very selective use of instrumental factors in making SPP decisions. The selection criteria are political, such as the ideology of politicians, their intention to reward their supporters and even themselves, the unwillingness of the public to pay for corrections, the culture of government organizations, and path-dependent behavioral patterns. For example, economic efficiency may have a different significance in different states. Comparatively, low-cost states, namely states that have the least potential of obtaining cost savings through the use of SPP, are more enthusiastic in cost reduction through using SPP. This counterintuitive phenomenon can only be explained by the coexistence of low per inmate correctional costs and high conservatism, the latter of which drives the enthusiasm in cost savings, even at a feeble margin. Overcrowding also attracts more attention in the "get tough on crime" states that fear the intervention of the federal courts. In the long run, the politics-driven instrumental arguments may fail to realize their bold promises. The theoretical and empirical literature reviewed in Chapter 2 shows that SPP does not really provide much potential for cost savings for the government. The bold claims by SPP advocates that SPP brings about large cost savings and vast flexibility to governments are highly unreliable.[1] SPP decisions are made with the expectation of cost savings, yet it is common that "requirements for rigorous evaluation are not written into the contracts for prisons" (Camp and Gaes, 2001, p.288). Florida legislatively requires a 7% operating cost savings from SPP. However, only private prison firms, including Corrections Corporation of American, provide self-reported evidence of cost savings at the mandated level.[2] It is also hard to conclude that SPP makes a great contribution to the

[1] Scandals may discredit pro-SPP academic research. One major prison privatization researcher and advocate, Thomas Charles, was fined $20,000 by the Florida Ethics Commission because of his relationship with private prison firms. His research institute at Florida University was also forced to shut down by state officials (Nelson, 2002). This legal sanction can hardly be attributed to the ideological stance of Florida, which shows quite a support for SPP.

[2] Florida DOC argues that "all three privately managed adult prison facilities are more expensive than comparable publicly run facilities," in its Annual Report for the fiscal year 1996-97. Office of Program Policy Analysis and Government Accountability (OPPAGA) is required

reduction of overcrowding. Liberal states with highly overcrowded prison systems often refrain from using SPP, while private prisons in many conservative states may work to stimulate the production of prisoners by state governments.

These facts suggest that the instrumental justifications for SPP may prove to be futile in the long run, and may lead to future backlash on the real performance evaluation of SPP. In fact, in recent years the awful practice of some private prisons has dimmed the future growth of SPP. Some governments responded by canceling or stopping the renewal of SPP contracts, or restricting the future use of SPP. For example, in 2001 Washington DC removed its last prisoners from Northeast Ohio Correctional Centered, which is operated by CCA and is notorious for its history of escapes, violent assaults, stabbings, and homicides (Greene, 2003). Governments should be more cautious in evaluating the economic efficiency of SPP, in using economic justifications, and in balancing the short-term benefits and the long-term costs. Future research should bring about more evidence to compare the cost efficiency between prisoner outsourcing and public warehousing. Such comparison should be based not on the change of the aggregate correctional budgets, but on per inmate operating cost (PIOC). Since many non-SPP states have high PIOC, it is of particular interest to investigate how much these states might save through SPP. If these states will not save much money, it will be especially interesting to determine the political factors that raise the cost of using private custody for their prisoners. If they will, then it is meaningful to examine the political dynamics and the prison system of these states to identify the reasons for not using SPP.

My research suggests that governments should pay more attention to negative political and legal consequences of SPP. Because of the optimistic rhetoric that SPP reduces overcrowding, enhances prison service quality and saves money for taxpayers, the political risk of SPP tends to be underestimated, especially when the federal courts refrain from intervening and when private prisons gain local support by bringing about economic prosperity to local economies. Private prisons, by strategically imitating public prisons and avoiding direct competition for prisoners with public prisons, endeavor to embed themselves into the current political structures and institutions rather than to impose challenges. Yet, the political balance that SPP maintains may not be stable over time. SPP may hurt a set of political

---

by Florida state law to review the performance of privately run prison facilities and it also reaches similar conclusions (McDonald et al., 1998).

values and impose potential risks. Mainly, delegation of the authority to punish creates the risk of producing unaccountable state actors since private contractors are not subject to various public laws that impose procedural and substantive constraints and various obligations on public agencies. Who should a private contractor be accountable to, for what, and how? Should governments be accountable for the actions taken by private contractors? What if private prison employees strike or walk out in a legal way? [3] The unavoidable incompleteness of contracts, which can be very serious regarding the human service nature of corrections, provides discretion to private contractors who may benefit from opportunistic behaviors. Being private, they may not be disciplined or held accountable like public agencies. Additionally, their location outside the borders of the contracting state further increases the difficulty of contract management by reducing the possible remedial measures that state governments may take. These problems are made more difficult since governments may in fact want to become more flexible and avoid accountability through SPP. While governments can shift blame to private contractors, private contractors also have a chance to escape responsibility by claiming themselves to be acting as agents of the state.

Essentially, SPP endangers a fundamental political value: democratic governance and its rules in delegating public authority. This danger is not to be made innocuous even when SPP does bring about significant cost savings. Since it is impossible to make private contractors publicly accountable in the literal sense without converting them to government firms, it is necessary for governments to make arrangements to avoid the accountability vacuum. Governments can train themselves to be smart buyers by incorporating managerial talents in contract-making, monitoring and evaluation. They can also deal with contractual incompleteness by imposing regulations. Yet although ex ante preventive measures can reduce the odds of contractual hazards, they are cost-adding and may harm the very purpose of privatization. A promising research issue is to investigate the real arrangement of accountability sharing under SPP, to identify the happenings in private prisons that governments are still accountable for, to identify the actual shedding of accountability to the private sector, and to identify the loss of accountability.

---

[3] According to *National Labor Relations Act*, it is unlawful for an employer or governments to interfere with the rights of workers to strike. Yet public employees are specifically excluded from this right (Logan, 1990). In 1996, Justice Department reversed its plans for using private contractors to operate the facilities identified in its 1996 and 1997 budget proposals because of its worry about this risk (GAO, 1996).

My research also shows that SPP faces resistance from the traditional Weberian state and may not have the potential to achieve a dominant role in corrections in the long run. SPP has lost its momentum in recent years and stepped into a stage of stagnation. Resistance to SPP is not just from correctional unions and workers, but also from other veto-players whose interests are threatened by the political and legal consequences of SPP. SPP greatly risks the public authority by sharing the power of imprisonment with private firms. It imposes serious doubt on the boundary between the state and the society. As a response, governments often consciously set quantitative and structural constraints to protect their ultimate control on punishment and to prevent legal and political crises. Imprisonment is further divided and classified to have core (maximum security prisons) and non-core components. Private prisons are rarely operated as maximum security facilities. Also, the nationwide SPP level is limited to such a low level (around 6%) that most state governments still have the capacity to independently make penal policies and govern prison contractors. It is highly possible that governments treat this kind of privatization as a makeshift strategy. Policy bandwagon effects may exist. This prudent practice makes it possible for governments to reverse SPP practices, as is true at least for the 10 swing states identified in 2003. Correspondingly, it is meaningful to analyze how state governments deal with the "hollowing out" problem by consciously making strategic plans and regulating the development of SPP. For those with high SPP levels, such as New Mexico, and those with a high number of prisoners outsourced, such as Texas, case studies can produce valuable information. Also, it is important to look at the privatization of other core governmental functions to disclose the patterned differences and/or similarity between SPP and other core functions, with a purpose to do generalization.

My research shows that state governments, public prison systems, and prison markets are aware of the different nature of SPP to that of service-contracting. Such consensus makes extended privatization a default form of SPP and determines the basic momentum for the continuous development of SPP: the continuous increase of prisoners. It is of vital importance for the private prison industry to support tougher crime control and stricter constraints on public capital investment on prisons.[4] Another self-protection strategy of the private prison industry is to use long-term contracts with risk-sharing

---

[4] To be impartial, correctional officers' unions are also active in promoting tougher crime control policies and advocating expanding prison systems, in order for enlarged political power and public expenditures. This determines that public unions and private prison firms are two conflicting members of the same prison industrial complex.

provisions to hedge the risk of prisoner shortages in the future. This has to create a dilemma for governments that are highly dependent on SPP when the number of prisoners decreases. Governments may be obliged to deliver prisoners to contractors while having a public prison system not fully used. The worst thing is that governments may be pushed by the interests of public and private prisons to be productive in imposing punishment. This raises several research interests. It is of importance to investigate the lobbying efforts of the private prison industry and their effects on SPP, to measure the possible "moral hazards" of private contractors, [5] to investigate the contractual arrangements on payment and risk-sharing, and to design contingent solutions to another "crisis": the deflation of prisoner population. It would be interesting to explore the influence of SPP on prisoner populations.

Finally, my research suggests that current policy debates on SPP may be of secondary importance. SPP may be problematic, but originally it was intended as a solution to the problems of state correctional systems, such as the unconstitutional overcrowding and the unreasonably high per capita correctional cost citizens have to burden. What is often ignored is that these problems were derived from the changes in criminal justice policies. By emphasizing individual rational choice and individual responsibility but ignoring the social conditions that give rise to criminal behavior, conservative social control policies shed the social responsibility of governments, abandoned the rehabilitative goals and resorted to severe punishment, consequently creating the functional dilemmas in correctional administration, and finally led to the relevance of SPP. As a result, problems of SPP reflect problems of the whole criminal justice system. Current debates on SPP fall short of discussing the fundamental policy issue (ref. Wood, 2003; Sinden, 2003). This certainly limits the horizon of SPP debates, produces simplistic projections of prisoner populations and of the demand for private prisons, and thus fails to consider directional changes. Clearly, cost savings and sound prison management are valuable, yet if the ultimate goal is to control the budget, reduce per resident correctional cost, and alleviate prison overcrowding, then it is indispensable to control the input of the prisoner population, in other words, to relax the tough crime control policies. Undoubtedly, underlying the budget explosion of corrections are certain conservative values, which treat criminal behavior as individual's rational

---

[5] For example, due to conflict of interests, private prisons may have an incentive to reduce rehabilitative programs, to spend insufficiently on security and medical care, or to make prisoners stay longer.

choice rather than a product of social conditions. So alternatively, governments should think about the option to return to the rehabilitative model of corrections. Going back to the logic of the privatization of core functions, it shows that policy analysis and policy making regarding SPP have to take the political dynamics as a fundamental beginning point, not vice versa.

# BIBLIOGRAPHY

Alexander, Elizabeth. 2003. "Private prisons and health care: the HMO from hell". In *Capitalist punishment: prison privatization and human rights.* Edited by Andrew Coyle, Allison Campbell, and Rodney Neufeld. Atlanta: Clarity Press, Inc. London: Zed Books.

Ali, Abbas. 2004. "Job outsourcing." *International Journal of Commerce & Management,* Vol. 14 Issue 1, pp, i-iii

Allison, Graham. 1999. "Public and private management: Are they fundamentally alike in all unimportant respects?" In *Current issues in public administration.* Edited by Frederick Lane. Boston: Bedford/St. Martin's.

Amemiya, T. 1973. "Regression analysis when the dependent variables are truncated normal". *Econometrica,* 41, 997-1016

Ammons, D and King, C. 1984. "Local government professionalism." *The Bureaucrat* 13: 52-57

Austin, James and Garry Coventry. 2001. *Emerging issues on privatized prisons.* Bureau of Justice Assistance

Baker, Bruce. "Receipts and expenditures of state governments and of local governments, 1959-2001." In *Survey of current business.* June 2003. Department of Commerce.

Bales, William; Laura Bedard; Susan Quinn; David Ensley; Glen Holley; Alan Duffee; Stephanie Sanford. 2003. *Recidivism: an analysis of public and private state prison releases in Florida.* Florida Department of Corrections. December, 2003. http://www.dc.state.fl.us/pub/recidivismfsu/

Bates, E. 1998. "Over the next 5 years analysts expect the private share of the prison market to more than double." *The Nation.* 11.

Beccaria, Cesare. 1986. *On crimes and punishments.* Translated by David Young. Indianapolis, IN: Hackett Pub.

Becker, Fred and A.J. Mackelprang. 1990. "Attitudes of state legislators toward contracting for public service." *American Review of Public Administration.* Vol. 20, No. 3 September, 1990. pp175-189

Behn, Robert and Peter Kant. 1999. "Strategies for avoiding the pitfalls of performance contracting". *Public Productivity and Management Review.* 22(4), pp470-489

Belbot, Barbara. 2004. "Report on the Prison Litigation Reform Act: what have the courts decided so far?" *The Prison Journal* Vol. 84, Issue. 3, September 2004. pp. 290-316.

Bernstein, Jared; Elizabeth McNichol; Laurence Mishel; and Robert Rahradnik. 2000.

*Pulling apart: a state-by-state analysis of income trends,* Washington DC: Economic Policy Institute and the Center for Budget and Policy Priorities.

Berry, Frances and William Berry. 1999. "Innovation and diffusion models in policy research," In *Theories of the policy process* Edited by Paul A. Sabatier. Boulder, Colo: Westview Press, 1999

Bureau of Justice Statistics (BJS). 1993. *Survey of state prison inmates, 1991 .*

_____ . 1996. *Sourcebook of criminal justice statistics, 1995.*

_____ . 1999. *State prison expenditures, 1996..*

_____ . 2000a. *Prisoners in 1999.*

_____ . 2000b. *Sourcebook of Criminal Justice Statistics, 1999.*

_____ . 2001. *Prisoners in 2000.*

_____ . 2002a. *Prisoners in 2001.*

_____ . 2002b. *Recidivism of Prisoners Released in 1994.*

_____ . 2003a. *Census of State and Federal Correctional Facilities, 2000 .*

_____ . 2003b. *Prisoners in 2002.*

_____ . 2004a. *Prisoners in 2003.*

_____ . 2004b. *State prison expenditures, 2001.*

_____ . 2004c. *Sourcebook of criminal justice statistics, 2002.*

_____ . 2005. *Prison and jail inmates at midyear 2004*

Borjas, George. 2003. "The wage structure and the sorting of workers into the public sector." In *For the people: can we fix public service?* Edited by John D. Donahue and Joseph S. Nye. Cambridge, Mass; Washington, DC: Brookings Institution Press.

Bowker, Lee. 1983. "Problems and prospects." In *Encyclopedia of crime and justice* Sanford Kadish, Edited by Sanford Kadish. New York: Free Press. V.3, 1983.

Bowman, Gary; Simon Hakim; and Paul Seidenstat. 1992. "Introduction" to *Privatizing the United States justice system: police, adjudication, and corrections services from the private sector*. Edited by Gary Bowman, Simon Hakim, and Paul Seidenstat. N.C: McFarland & Co.

Bozeman, Barry. 1987. *All organizations are public: bridging public and private organizational theories*. San Francisco: Jossey-Bass.

Brown, Trevor and Matt Potoski. 2003. "Transaction costs and institutional explanations for government service production decisions." *Journal of Public Administration Research & Theory* 13: 441-468.

Bureau of the Census. 2004. Web: www.census.gov

Bureau of Labor Statistics. 2004. *Union Members in 2003*.

Camp, Camille and George Camp. 2000. *The 2000 correctional yearbook: private prison*. Connecticut: Criminal Justice Institute, Inc.

Camp, Scott and Gerald Gaes. 2001. "Private adult prisons: what do we really know and why do not we know more." In *Privatization of criminal justice: Past Present and Future* Edited by David Shichor and Michael Gilbert. Cincinnati: Anderson.

Clark, John. 1998. *Report to the Attorney General: inspection and review of Northeast Ohio Correctional Center*. Washington, DC: Office of the Corrections Trustee for the District of Columbia.

Clear, Todd and George Cole. 1990. *American corrections*. Pacific Grove, CA: Brooks/Cole Pub.

Clingermayer, James and Dan Wood. 1995. "Disentangling patterns of state debt financing." *The American Political Science Review*, Vol. 89, No. 1 (Mar., 1995) PP108-120

Crip, Clair. 1997. *Legal aspects of correctional management*. Gaithersburg, MD: Aspen Publishers.

Crants, Doctor. 1991. "Private prison management: a study in economic efficiency." *Journal of Contemporary Criminal Justice* 7(1), 49-59

Crouch, Ben and James Marquart. 1989. *An appeal to justice: litigated reform of Texas prisons*. Austin: University of Texas Press

Crown, William. 1997. *Statistical models for the social and behavioral sciences: multiple regression and limited-dependent variable models*. Westport, Conn: Praeger

Cummings, Stephen. 1998. *The dixification of America: the American odyssey into the conservative economic trap* Westport, Conn: Praeger.

DeHoog, Ruth. 1984. *Contracting out for human services: economic, political, and organizational perspectives*. Albany: State University of New York Press.

DiMaggio, P. and W. Powell. 1983. "The iron cage revisited: institutional isomorphism and collective rationality in organizational fields," *American Sociological Review* 2: 147-160

Donahue, John. 1988. *Prisons for profit: public justice, private interests.* Economic Policy Institute. Washington, DC.

_____ . 1989. *The privatization decision: public ends, private means.* New York: Basic Books.

Downs, Anthony. 1967. *Inside bureaucracy.* Boston: Little Brown.

Duffee, David. 1983. "Careers in criminal justice: corrections." In *Encyclopedia of crime and justice.* Edited by Sanford Kadish. New York: Free Press.

Durham III, Alexis. 1993. "The future of correctional privatization: lessons from the past." In *Privatizing correctional institutions.* Edited by Gary Bowman, Simon Hakim, and Paul Seidenstat. New Brunswick and London: Transaction Publishers

Elazar, Daniel. 1966. *American Federalism: A View from the States.* New York: Thomas Y. Crowell.

Erikson, Robert; Gerald Wright; and John McIver. 1987. "State political culture and public opinion." *American Political Science Review.* Vol.81 No.3 PP797-813

_____ . 1989. "Political parties, public opinion, and state policy in the United States." *The American Political Science Review.* Vol. 83, No. 3 (Sep., 1989), 729-750

_____ . 1993. *Statehouse democracy.* Cambridge; New York: Cambridge University Press.

Farabee, D., and Knight, Kevin. 2002. *A comparison of public and private prisons in Florida: During- and post-prison performance indicators.* Los Angeles, CA: Query Research.

Fenton, John. 1957. *Politics in the border states.* New Orleans: Hauser

Florida Corrections Commission. 1996. "An assessment of Florida's privatization of state prisons" *1996 Annual Report* November 1, 1996

Freeman, Jody. 2002. "Extending public law norms through privatization." *Harvard Law Review*, Vol. 116

Freeman, Richard and Casey Ichniowski. 1988. "Introduction: the public sector look of American unionism." In *When public sector workers unionize* Edited by Richard Freeman and Casey Ichniowski. Chicago: University of Chicago Press

Frendreis John and Laura Vertz. 1988. "A model of decision making and the public service professional." *Political Behavior.* Vol. 10, No. 1, PP77-93

GAO. 1991. *Government contractors: are service contractors performing inherently governmental functions?* GAO reports, GGD-92-11. Washington, November 1991.

_____. 1996. *Private and public prisons: studies comparing operational costs and/or quality of service.* GAO/GGD-96-158. August, 1996

_____. 2003. *Defense management: DOD faces challenges implementing its core competency approach and A-76 competitions.* GAO report GAO-03-818.

Gettinger, Stephen. 1982. "Accreditation on trial." *Corrections Magazine.* February 1982, pp. 6-21, 51-55

Gilmour, Robert and Jensen, Laura. 1998. "Reinventing government accountability: Public functions, privatization, and the meaning of 'state action." *Public Administration Review*, May/Jun98, Vol. 58 Issue 3, p247, 12p

Gormley, William. 1999. "Privatization revisited." In *Current issues in public administration.* Edited by Frederick Lane. Boston: Bedford/St. Martin's.

Gray, Virginia. 1973. "Innovation in the States: A Diffusion Study" *The American Political Science Review*, Vol. 67, No. 4. (Dec., 1973), pp. 1174-1185.

Greene, Jeffrey. 2002. *Cities and privatization: prospects for the new century.* Upper Saddle River, N.J: Prentice Hall.

Greene, Judith. 2000. "Prison Privatization: Recent Developments in the United States". Paper presented at the International Conference on Penal Abolition.

_____. 2003. "Lack of correctional services". In *Capitalist punishment: prison privatization and human rights.* Edited by Andrew Coyle; Allison Campbell; and Rodney Neufeld. Atlanta: Clarity Press, Inc. London: Zed Books.

Greene, William. 1990. *Econometric analysis.* New York: Macmillan; London: Collier Macmillan.

Gregory, Robert. 1995. "Accountability, responsibility and corruption: Managing the 'public production process'." In *The State Under Contract*, Edited by Jonathan Boston. Wellington, New Zealand.

Gunderson, Morley. 1974. "Training subsidies and disadvantaged workers: regression with a limited dependent variable." *The Canadian Journal of Economics*, Vol.7, No.4 (Nov, 1974), 611-624.

Hallinan, Joseph. 2001. *Going up the river: travels in a prison nation.* New York: Random House.

Handler, Joel. 1996. *Down from bureaucracy: the ambiguity of privatization and empowerment*. Princeton, N.J: Princeton University Press.

Hanke, Steve. 1985. "The Theory of Privatization." In *The privatization option: a strategy to shrink the size of government*. Edited by Stuart Butler. The Heritage Foundation.

Hanson, Roger and Daley, Henry. 1994. *Challenging the conditions of prisons and jails: a report on Section 1983 Litigation*. US. Department of Justice. December, 1994 92-BJ-CX-K026.

Hart, Oliver; Andrei Shleifer; and Robert Vishny. 1997. "The proper scope of government: theory and an application to prisons." *The Quarterly Journal of Economics*, Vol.112, No.4 (Nov., 1997), 1127-1161.

Helms, Ronald and David Jacobs. 2002. "The political context of sentencing: an analysis of community and individual determinants," *Social Forces*. Vol. 81, No.2 (Dec, 2002), 577-604.

Hirsch, Barry and David Macpherson. 1995 and 2000. *Union Membership and Coverage Database* Based on the Current Population Survey by Bureau of Labor Statistics http://www.unionstats.com

Hirsch, Barry and John Addison. 1986. *Economic analysis of unions: new approaches and evidence*. Boston: Allen & Unwin

Hirsch, Werner. 1995. "Factors Important in Local Governments Privatization Decisions," *Urban Affairs Review*, Vol. 31, No. 2, pp. 226-243.

Hodge, Graeme. 2000. *Privatization: an international review of performance*. Boulder, CO: Westview Press.

Hughes, Everett. 1965. "Professions." In *The professions in America*. Edited by Kenneth Lynn. Boston" Houghton Mifflin.

Hyman, David. 1987. *Public finance: a contemporary application of theory to policy* Chicago: Dryden Press.

Ikenberry, John. 1990. "The international spread of privatization policies: inducements, learning, and 'policy bandwagoning'." In *The Political Economy of Public Sector Reform and Privatization*. Edited by Suleiman, E. and Waterbury, J. Boulder, CO: Westview Press.

Jacobs, James. 1983. *New Perspectives on Prisons and Imprisonment* Ithaca, NY: Cornell University Press.

Kerle, Ken. 1999. "Jails as Long-Term Facilities." In *Prison and Jail Administration: Practice and Theory* Edited by Peter Carlson and Judith Garrett. MD: Aspen Publishers.

Kettl, Donald. 1993. *Sharing power: public governance and private markets*. Washington, DC: The Brookings Institution.

Knepper, Paul. 1991. "A Brief History of Profiting From the Punishment of Crime." Paper presented at the 50th anniversary meeting of the American Society of Criminology, San Francisco, November.

Langbein, Laura. 1986. "Money and access: some empirical evidence." *The Journal of Politics*. Vol. 48, No.4 (Nov, 1986), 1052-1062.

Lanza-Kaduce, L., Parker, K. F., and Thomas, C. W. 1999. "A comparative recidivism analysis of releasees from private and public prisons." *Crime and Delinquency*, 45(1), 28-47.

Lanza-Kaduce, L., and Maggard, S. 2001. *The long-term recidivism of public and private prisoners*. A paper presented that the National Conference of the BJS and Justice Research and Statistics Association in New Orleans.

Lawrence, Sarah and Jeremy Travis. 2004. *The New Landscape of Imprisonment: Mapping America's Prison Expansion*. Research report of Justice Policy Center of Urban Institute. April, 2004.

Leblanc, Clif. 2001. "Prisons might lose accreditation." URL: http://www.thestate.com/mld/ thestate/news/5628651.htm

Leonard, Herman. 1990. "Private Time: The Political Economy of Private Prison Finance." In *Private Prisons and the Public Interest*. Edited by Douglas McDonald. New Brunswick: Rutgers University Press.

Lewis, Gregg. 1988. "Union/Nonunion Wage Gaps in the Public Sector." In *When public sector workers unionize* Edited by Richard Freeman and Casey Ichniowski. Chicago: University of Chicago Press.

Levitt, Steven. 1996. "The Effect of Prison Population Size on Crime Rates: Evidence from Prison Overcrowding Litigation." *The Quarterly Journal of Economics*, Vol.111, No.2, pp319-351.

Light, Paul. 1999. *The true size of government*. Washington, DC: Brookings Institution.

Lindblom, Charles.1959. "The Science of 'Muddling Through'", *Public Administration Review* Vol. 19, pp79-88.

Logan, Charles. 1990. *Private prisons: cons and pros*. New York: Oxford University Press.

Mackenize, Doris. 2001. "Sentencing and Corrections in the 21st Century: Setting the Stage for the Future." Report submitted to US. Department of Justice.

March, James and Johan Olsen. 1983. "Organizing Political Life: What administrative Reorganization Tells Us about Government." *The American Political Science Review*, Vol. 77, No. 2. (Jun., 1983), pp. 281-296.

Mariner, Joanne. 2004. "Private contractors who torture." FindLaw Columnist. CNN.com.   June   17,   2004.   http://www.cnn.com/2004/LAW/ 06/17/mariner.contractors.

McDonald, Douglas.1990. "When Government fails: Going Private as a Last Resort." In *Private Prisons and the Public Interest*. Edited by Douglas McDonald. New Brunswick: Rutgers University Press.

McDonald, Douglas; Fournier, Elizabeth; Russell-Einhourn, Malcolm; and Crawford, Stephen. 1998. *Private prisons in the United State: an assessment of current practice*. Document of Abt Associates Inc.

McDonald, Douglas and Carl Patten. 2003. *Government's management of private prisons*. Abt Associates Inc report. Cambridge, Mass.

McDonald, John and Moffitt, Robert. 1980. "The Uses of Tobit Analysis." *Review* of *Economics & Statistics*. May80, Vol. 62 Issue 2, p318, 4p.

McDowell, Allen and Nicholas Cox. 2004. "Logit transformation". http://www.stata.com/
support/faqs/stat/logit.html

Meyer, John and Brian Rowan. 1977. "Institutionalized Organizations: Formal Structure as Myth and Ceremony," *American Journal of Sociology*, 83: 340-363.

Milward, Brinton. 1994. "Implications of contracting out: New roles for the hollow state." In *New Paradigms for Government: Issues for the Changing Public Service*. Edited by Ingraham, P. and Romzek, B. San Francisco, CA: Josey-Bass.

Moe, Ronald. 1987. "Exploring the limits of privatization." *Public Administration Review*. Nov/Dec, Vol. 47, No. 6. pp453-460.

Mosher, Frederick. 1968. *Democracy and the public service*. New York: Oxford University Press.

Nagel, I. 1990. "Structuring sentencing discretion: the new federal sentencing guidelines," *Journal of Criminal Law & Criminology* 80 (1990): 883, 913-939.

Nathan, Stephen. 2002. "The prison industry goes global." From Yes! Magazine. http://grassrootsleadership.org/Articles/article3_spr2002.html

National   Conference   of   State   Legislatures.   2004.   Web   URL: http://www.ncsl.org/programs/
fiscal/tels2004.htm

Nelson, Julianne. 1998. "Comparing public and private prison costs." In *Private prisons in the United States: An assessment of current practice* Edited by D. McDonald, E. Fournier, M. Russell-Einhorn, & S. Crawford. Boston: Abt Associates Inc.

National Institute of Corrections. 1996. *Privatization and Contracting in Corrections: Results of an NIC Survey.* Longmont, Colorado.

National Opinion Research Center. 2003. *General Social Surveys, 1972-2002* Storrs, CT: The Roper Center for Public Opinion Research, University of Connecticut.

National Performance Review. 1993. *From red tape to results: creating a government that works better and costs less* Government Printing Office, September 1993.

Nelson, Robert. 2003. "Think more private prisons would be good for Arizona? Think again, sucker." Big House Inc. http://www.phoenixnewtimes.com/issues/2003-04-03/news/feature_print.html

Neter, John; Michael Kutner; Christopher Nachtsheim; and William Wasserman. 1996. *Applied linear statistical models* Chicago: Irwin

Nicholson-Crotty, Sean. 2004. "The Politics and Administration of Privatization: Contracting Out for Corrections Management in the United States." *Policy Studies Journal*, 2004, Vol. 32 Issue 1, p41, 17p

Niskanen, William. 1971. *Bureaucracy and Representative Government.* Chicago: Aldine and Atherton.

Oates, Wallace. 1985. "Searching for Leviathan: An Empirical Study" *The American Economic Review*, Vol. 75, No. 4. pp748-757.

Office of Management and Budget (OMB). 1999. *Circular No. A-76* (Revised).

Overbeck, Charles. 1997. "Prison Factories Slave Labor for the New World Order?" http://www.meta-religion.com/Secret_societies/Conspiracies/Economy/prison_factories.htm

Papke, Leslie and Jeffrey Wooldridge. 1996. "Econometric methods for fractional response variables with an application to 401 (K) plan participation rates". *Journal of Applied Economics*. Vol. 11, No. 6 (Nov. – Dec., 1996), pp619-632

Parenti, Christian. 2000. *Lockdown America: police and prisons in the age of crisis.* London; New York: Verso.

_____ . 2003. "Privatized problems: for-profit incarceration in trouble". In *Capitalist Punishment: Prison Privatization and Human Rights.* Edited by Andrew Coyle; Allison Campbell; and Rodney Neufeld. Atlanta: Clarity Press, Inc. London: Zed Books.

Pierson, Paul. 1994. *Dismantling the welfare state? : Reagan, Thatcher, and the politics of retrenchment* Cambridge, England; New York : Cambridge University Press

_____ . 2000. "Increasing Returns, Path Dependence, and the Study of Politics" *American Political Science Review*, Jun2000, Vol. 94 Issue 2, p251, 17p

Pike, John. 1997. "Lorton Correction Complex." http://www.fas.org/ irp/imint/lorton.htm

Poulson, Barry. 2004. *Tax and spending limits: Theory, Analysis, and Policy.* Independent Institute. www.IndependenceInstitute.org

Price, Byron. 2002. *Economics, ideology, politics, and profits: what drives prison privatization?* Dissertation at Mississippi State University.

Salamon, Lester. 1989. "The Changing Tools of Government Action: An overview." In *Beyond Privatization: the Tools of Government Action*, edited by Lester Salamon Washington, DC: Urban Institute Press.

Savas, Emanuel. 1987. *Privatization*. Chatham, N.J.: Chatham House Publishers.

_____ 2000. *Privatization and Public-Private Partnerships*. New York: Chatham House.

Schlosser, Eric. 1998. "The prison-industrial complex." *The Atlantic Monthly.* December, 1998.

Sclar, Elliott. 2000. *You do not always get what you pay for: the economics of privatization*. Ithaca, N.Y: Cornell University Press.

Sentencing Project and Human Rights Watch. 1998. *Losing the Vote: the impact of felony disenfranchisement laws in the United States.*

Shapiro, Andrew. 1993. "Challenging criminal disenfranchisement under the voting rights act: A new strategy." 103 *Yale Law Journal*. Nov, 1993.

Sharkansky, Ira. 1970. Regionalism *in American Politics*. New York: Bobbs-Merrill.

Shepherd, William. 1979. *The economics of industrial organization* Englewood Cliffs, N.J: Prentice-Hall.

Shichor, David. 1995. *Punishment for profit: private prisons/public concerns* Thousand Oaks, Cal: Sage Publications.

Sinden, Jeff. 2003. "The problem of prison privatization: the US experience". ." In *Capitalist Punishment: Prison Privatization and Human Rights.* Edited by Andrew Coyle; Allison Campbell; and Rodney Neufeld. Atlanta: Clarity Press, Inc. London: Zed Books.

Singer, Peter. 2003. *Corporate warriors: the rise of the privatized military industry*. Ithaca: Cornell University Press.

Singal, Alex and Raymond Reed. 1997. *An overview of the private corrections industry: Industry Analysis*. Baltimore, MD: Legg Mason Wood Walker, Inc.

Slyke, David. 2003. "The Mythology of Privatization in Contracting for Social Services." *Public Administration Review*, May/Jun2003, Vol. 63 Issue 3, p296

Starr, Paul. 1990. "The new life of the liberal state: privatization and the restructuring of state-society relations." In *The Political economy of public sector reform and privatization*. Edited by Suleiman, E. and Waterbury, J. 1990. Boulder, CO: Westview Press

Stillman, Richard. 1996. *The American bureaucracy: the core of modern government* Chicago: Nelson-Hall Publishers.

Thomas, Charles; Dianne Bolinger; and John Badalamenti. 1997. *Private adult correctional facility census, tenth edition*. Gainesville: University of Florida.

Thompson, James. 1967. *Organizations in action: social science bases of administrative theory*. New York, McGraw-Hill

Tilly, Charles. 1985. "War making and state making as organized crime," in *Bringing the state back in*, Peter B. Evans, Dietrich Rueschemeyer, Theda Skocpol, eds. Cambridge: Cambridge University Press.

_____ . 1992. *Coercion, capital, and European states, AD 990-1992*, Cambridge, MA: Blackwell.

_____ . 2003. *The politics of collective violence*. Cambridge, U.K; New York: Cambridge University Press.

Tobin, James. 1958. "Estimation of relationships for limited dependent variables." *Econometrica*. Vol. 26, No. 1 (Jan, 1958), 24-36

Tolbert, P. S. and L. G. Zucker. 1999. "The institutionalization of institutional theory," in S. R. Clegg and C. Hardy (eds.), *Studying organization: theory and method*. London: Sage Publications.

Toren, Nina. 1976. "Bureaucracy and professionalism: a reconciliation of Weber's thesis." *The Academy of Management Review*, Vol.1, No.3, PP36-46

Tullock, Gordon. 1965. *The politics of bureaucracy*. Washington, DC: Public Affairs Press.

Weber, Max. 1946. *From Max Weber: essays in sociology*. Translated, edited and introduced by Gerth, H. H. and C. Wright Mills. New York, Oxford University Press.

Wildavsky, Aaron, "Comprehensive versus incremental budgeting in the Department of Agriculture," *Administrative Science Quarterly* 10 (December 1965): 321-346.

Williamson, Oliver. 1975. *Markets and hierarchies, analysis and antitrust implications: a study in the economics of internal organization.* New York: Free Press

Wood, Philip. 2003. "The rise of the prison industrial complex in the United States." In *Capitalist punishment: prison privatization and human rights.* Edited by Andrew Coyle; Allison Campbell; and Rodney Neufeld. Atlanta: Clarity Press, Inc. London: Zed Books.

Yackle, Larry. 1989. *Reform and regret: the story of federal judicial involvement in the Alabama prison system.* New York: Oxford University Press

Yarden, David. 1994. "Prisons, profits, and the private sector solution." *American Journal of Criminal Law.* Vol.21 No. 1: 325-334

Zielbauer, Paul. 2005. "As health care in jails goes private: 10 days can be a death sentence." *New York Times.* February 27, 2005

# APPENDICES

## APPENDIX A. EMPIRICAL RESEARCH COMPARING PER INMATE OPERATING COSTS BETWEEN PUBLIC AND PRIVATE PRISONS

| Location of the facilities | Research period | Public facilities | | Private facilities | | SPP effect |
|---|---|---|---|---|---|---|
| | | No. | Daily PIOC ($) | No. | Daily PIOC ($) | |
| Texas | 1990 | Hypothetical | 42.7-43.13 | 4 | 36.76 | Positive |
| California | 1991-1992 | 2 | 36.15 45.55 | 1 | 42.68 | Mixed |
| Tennessee | July 1993-june 1994 | 2 | 34.9 35.45 | 1 | 35.39 | Mixed |
| Louisiana (1) | July 1995-june 1996 | 1 | 23.55 | 2 | 23.75 23.34 | Mixed |
| Louisiana (2) | 1992-1996 | 1 | 26.6 | 2 | 22.93 23.49 | Positive |
| Arizona | 1996 | 1 | 43.08 | 15 | 35.9 | Positive |

Source: GAO (1996), McDonald et al. (1998)

# APPENDIX B. CONVICTION-BASED DISENFRANCHISEMENT STATE LEGISLATION

| | Prison | Probation | Parole | Ex-felons | | Prison | Probation | Parole | Ex-felons |
|---|---|---|---|---|---|---|---|---|---|
| **Northeast** | | | | | **South** | | | | |
| Connecticut | X | X | X | | Alabama | X | X | X | X |
| Maine | | | | | Arkansas | X | X | X | |
| Massachusetts | | | | | Delaware | X | X | X | X |
| New Hampshire | X | | | | Florida | X | X | X | X |
| New jersey | X | X | X | | Georgia | X | X | X | |
| New York | X | | X | | Kentucky | X | X | X | X |
| Pennsylvania | X | | | | Louisiana | X | | | |
| Rhode Island | X | X | X | | Maryland | X | X | X | X |
| Vermont | | | | | Mississippi | X | X | X | X |
| | | | | | North Carolina | X | X | X | |
| | | | | | Oklahoma | X | X | X | |
| | | | | | South Carolina | X | X | X | |
| | | | | | Tennessee | X | X | X | X |
| | | | | | Texas | X | X | X | X |
| | | | | | Virginia | X | X | X | X |
| | | | | | West Virginia | X | X | X | |
| **Midwest** | | | | | **West** | | | | |
| Illinois | X | | | | Alaska | X | X | X | |
| Indiana | X | | | | Arizona | X | X | X | X |
| Iowa | X | X | X | X | California | X | | X | |
| Kansas | X | | | | Colorado | X | | X | |
| Michigan | X | | | | Hawaii | X | | | |
| Minnesota | X | X | X | | Idaho | X | | | |
| Missouri | X | X | X | | Montana | X | | | |
| Nebraska | X | X | X | | Nevada | X | X | X | X |
| North Dakota | X | | | | New Mexico | X | X | X | X |
| Ohio | X | | | | Oregon | X | | | |

| South Dakota | X | | | Utah | | | | |
| Wisconsin | X | X | X | Washington | X | X | X | X |
| | | | | Wyoming | X | X | X | X |

## APPENDIX C. FEDERAL AND STATE PRISONERS IN PRIVATE FACILITIES IN 2002-2003

| Jurisdiction | 2003 | 2002 | SPP rate in 2003 | Jurisdiction | 2003 | 2002 | SPP rate in 2003 |
|---|---|---|---|---|---|---|---|
| US Total | 95,522 | 93,912 | 6.5 | South | 48,222 | 46,091 | 8.2 |
| | | | | Alabama | 1,698 | 0 | 5.8 |
| Federal | 21,865 | 20,274 | 12.6 | Arkansas | 0 | 0 | 0 |
| State | 73,657 | 73,638 | 5.7 | Delaware | 0 | 0 | 0 |
| | | | | Florida | 4,330 | 4,173 | 5.4 |
| Northeast | 3,201 | 3,146 | 1.8 | Georgia | 4,589 | 4,573 | 9.7 |
| Connecticut | 0 | 0 | 0 | Kentucky | 1,640 | 1,635 | 9.9 |
| Maine | 30 | 8 | 1.5 | Louisiana | 2,918 | 2,929 | 8.1 |
| Massachusetts | 0 | 0 | 0 | Maryland | 122 | 127 | 0.5 |
| New Hampshire | 0 | 0 | 0 | Mississippi | 3,463 | 3,435 | 14.9 |
| New Jersey | 2,636 | 2,601 | 9.7 | North Carolina | 215 | 186 | 0.6 |
| New York | 0 | 0 | 0 | Oklahoma | 6,022 | 6,470 | 26.4 |
| Pennsylvania | 535 | 537 | 1.3 | South Carolina | 44 | 21 | 0.2 |
| Rhode Island | 0 | 0 | 0 | Tennessee | 5,049 | 4,200 | 19.9 |
| Vermont/c | 0 | 0 | 0 | Texas | 16,570 | 16,773 | 9.9 |
| | | | | Virginia | 1,562 | 1,569 | 4.5 |
| Midwest | 4,957 | 6,748 | 2 | West Virginia | 0 | 0 | 0 |
| Illinois | 0 | 0 | 0 | | | | |
| Indiana | 652 | 843 | 2.8 | West | 17,277 | 17,653 | 6 |
| Iowa | 0 | 0 | 0 | Alaska | 1,386 | 1,360 | 30.6 |
| Kansas | 0 | 0 | 0 | Arizona | 2,323 | 1,965 | 7.5 |
| Michigan | 480 | 460 | 1 | California | 3,507 | 4,649 | 2.1 |
| Minnesota | 0 | 0 | 0 | Colorado | 3,013 | 2,452 | 15.3 |
| Missouri | 0 | 0 | 0 | Hawaii | 1,478 | 1,347 | 25.4 |
| Nebraska | 0 | 0 | 0 | Idaho | 1,267 | 1,266 | 21.5 |
| North Dakota | 0 | 23 | 0 | Montana | 1,059 | 963 | 29.3 |
| Ohio | 1,901 | 1,927 | 4.2 | Nevada | 0 | 434 | 0 |
| South Dakota | 25 | 32 | 0.8 | New Mexico | 2,751 | 2,690 | 44.2 |

| Wisconsin | 1,899 | 3,463 | 8.4 | Oregon | 0 | 0 | 0 |
|-----------|-------|-------|-----|--------|---|---|---|
| | | | | Utah | 0 | 0 | 0 |
| | | | | Washington | 0 | 0 | 0 |
| | | | | Wyoming | 493 | 527 | 26.3 |

## APPENDIX D. THE CORRELATION MATRIX OF INDEPENDENT VARIABLES

| | overcrowd | PCE | TSL | PIOC | Lib | Midwest | South | West | Union | Prof | Year | Court |
|---|---|---|---|---|---|---|---|---|---|---|---|---|
| Overcrowd | 1.00 | | | | | | | | | | | |
| PCE | -0.21 | 1.00 | | | | | | | | | | |
| TSL | -0.25 | .34(*) | 1.00 | | | | | | | | | |
| PIOC | -0.02 | -0.16 | -0.05 | 1.00 | | | | | | | | |
| Lib | 0.20 | 0.00 | -0.03 | .61(**) | 1.00 | | | | | | | |
| Midwest | .41(**) | -0.17 | -.30(*) | 0.04 | 0.12 | 1.00 | | | | | | |
| South | -.36(**) | .31(*) | 0.06 | -.58(**) | -.48(**) | -.39(**) | 1.00 | | | | | |
| West | -0.03 | 0.04 | .30(*) | 0.15 | -0.03 | -.33(*) | -.41(**) | 1.00 | | | | |
| Union | 0.20 | -0.17 | 0.00 | .70(**) | .81(**) | 0.06 | -.61(**) | 0.05 | 1.00 | | | |
| Prof | 0.24 | -0.08 | -0.06 | 0.26 | 0.18 | 0.06 | -.33(*) | 0.14 | 0.17 | 1.00 | | |
| Year | -0.23 | .33(*) | 0.19 | -0.21 | -.36(*) | -0.23 | 0.24 | 0.27 | -.40(**) | -0.09 | 1.00 | |
| Court | -0.27 | .43(**) | .31(*) | -0.05 | -0.24 | -0.13 | .35(*) | -0.12 | -0.28 | -0.11 | .29(*) | 1.00 |
| Prisoners | -0.09 | .62(**) | 0.19 | -0.23 | 0.11 | -0.09 | 0.22 | -0.07 | -0.01 | -0.10 | .41(**) | 0.25 |

* Significant at .05 level.

** Significant at .01 level (2-tailed).

# APPENDIX E. VARIANCE INFLATION FACTOR (VIF) COEFFICIENTS

|           | Collinearity Statistics | |
|-----------|-----------|-------|
|           | Tolerance | VIF   |
| Overcrowd | .630      | 1.588 |
| PCE       | .451      | 2.216 |
| TSL       | .660      | 1.515 |
| PIOC      | .269      | 3.720 |
| Lib       | .272      | 3.672 |
| Midwest   | .364      | 2.745 |
| South     | .172      | 5.819 |
| West      | .329      | 3.041 |
| Union     | .174      | 5.763 |
| Prof      | .809      | 1.236 |
| Years     | .505      | 1.981 |
| Court     | .579      | 1.728 |
| Prisoners | .389      | 2.572 |

Note: Dependent Variable is SPP level in 2003.

# APPENDIX F. AN INTRODUCTION TO THE TOBIT MODEL

The stochastic Tobit model is: $y = Max (0, Xb + U)$. $Xb + U$ is a latent linear index. For this model, the critical values of the index and the dependent variable are both arbitrarily chosen as 0. Error term U is assumed to be independently and normally distributed, $U \sim N(0\ s)$.

The task of the Tobit model is to explore the effect of X on Ey.

$Ey = 0.P(y=0) + E(y|y>0).P(y>0)$
$P(y>0) = P(Xb + U >0) = P(U>-Xb) = F(z)$

$z=Xb/s$, F is the cumulative normal distribution function.

Let's use $Ey^*$ to denote $E(y|y>0)$
So $Ey^* = E(y| Xb + U >0) = Xb + sf(z)/F(z)$

f(z) is the standard normal density function, $f(z)/F(z)$ is the inverse Mills Ratio. For the calculation of the expected value of censored data, see Greene (1990).

So $Ey = Ey^* \cdot F(z) = XbF(z) + sf(z)$

To analyze the effect of X on Ey, we can calculate the derivative of Ey on X.

$\partial Ey / \partial X = F(z) \cdot \partial Ey^* / \partial X + Ey^* \cdot \partial F(z) / \partial X$

There are two parts of the effect of X on Ey: (1) The change of the expected value of the nonlimit responses, weighted by the probability of having nonlimit responses; (2) The change of the probability of having nonlmit responses, weighted by the expected value of the nonlimit responses.

The derivatives in the above function can be obtained by:

$\partial Ey^* / \partial X = b [1 - zf(z)/F(z) - f(z)^2/F(z)^2]$

$\partial F(z) / \partial X = f(z)b/s$

So the total effect:

$\partial Ey / \partial X = F(z)b[1 - zf(z)/F(z) - f(z)^2/F(z)^2] + Ey^* f(z)b/s = bF(z)$

$\underbrace{\hspace{5cm}}$  $\underbrace{\hspace{2cm}}$

Part (1) effect        Part (2) effect

The estimation of the coefficient vector and the error term is obtained by using Maximum Likelihood estimation. The Likelihood function is unusual, obtained by multiplying the cumulative distribution function of the censored observations and the probability distribution function of the uncensored observations (Crown, 1997):

$L = IIF(b\ s)\ IIf(b\ s) = IIF(Xb/s)IIf[(y-Xb)/s]$

Amemiya (1973) proves that if the assumptions of the Tobit model hold, then the ML estimator will have the desirable properties. If the error term is not normal and homoscedastic, then the estimator will be nonconsistent. But this problem is generally not serious because of the specification of the index.

Interpretation of the Tobit results is a little tricky. The obtained Tobit coefficients have no straightforward interpretations beyond their sign and statistical significance, and their effects should be differentiated for the nonlimit and limit responses. For the nonlimit responses, the coefficient vector b does not indicate the marginal change of Ey, given one unit change of X. The marginal change of Ey is a proportion of b, namely bF(z), which is composed of two parts. One part is related to the change of the expected values of the nonlimit responses, Ey*, and another related to the change of the probability of having nonlimit responses, F(z). The proportions of these two parts are respectively: $1-zf(z)/F(z)- f(z)^2/F(z)^2$ and $zf(z)/F(z) + f(z)^2/F(z)^2$. For the limit response, change in X leads to the change of their probability of having nonlimit responses.

Influence of X on Ey is nonlinear and contingent on the value of F(z). Generally, we can use the average of X to find the average probability to have nonlimit responses and use it as a reference point to explore the effect of X on Ey and F(z). In practice, the rule of thumb is to use the proportion of nonlimit responses in the sample as a point value of F(z). For the prediction purpose, the expected probability to be nonlimit responses is F(z), while the expected value of the response is Ey = Ey*. F(z) = XbF(z) + sf(z).

# APPENDIX G. AN ILLUSTRATION OF THE DECOMPOSITION OF TOBIT EFFECTS

| Variables | ΔX | Tobit effect: ΔEy | Part I effect | | Part II effect | |
|---|---|---|---|---|---|---|
| | | | Amount | Fraction | Amount | Fraction |
| Overcrowding 95 | 1 percent | 0.21 | 0.09 | | 0.12 | |
| PCE 96 | 1 percent | 0.77 | 0.33 | | 0.45 | |
| TSL 95 | 0 to 1 | 1.89 | 0.80 | | 1.10 | |
| PIOC 96 | $1000 | 0.26 | 0.11 | 42% | 0.15 | 58% |
| State policy liberalism | 1 | -3.07 | -1.30 | | -1.78 | |
| Midwest | 0-1 | -1.11 | -0.47 | | -0.64 | |
| South | 0 to 1 | 6.02 | 2.55 | | 3.49 | |
| West | 0 to 1 | 6.44 | 2.72 | | 3.73 | |

| Professionalism 2000 | 1 percent | 0.13 | 0.06 | | 0.08 | |
| Year | 1 year | 0.99 | 0.42 | | 0.58 | |
| Court orders 95 | 1 order | -0.17 | -0.07 | | -0.10 | |
| State prisoners 2003 | 1000 prisoners | -0.05 | -0.02 | | -0.03 | |

Note: Calculation is according to McDonald and Moffitt.

# APPENDIX H. LOGISTICS RESULTS OF SPP DATA

a. Omnibus tests of model coefficients

| | Chi-square | df | Sig. |
| --- | --- | --- | --- |
| Step | 43.617 | 12 | .000 |
| Block | 43.617 | 12 | .000 |
| Model | 43.617 | 12 | .000 |

b. Model summary

| Step | -2 Log likelihood | Cox & Snell R-square | Nagelkerke R-square |
| --- | --- | --- | --- |
| 1 | 23.68 | .58 | .787 |

c. Coefficients

| | B | S.E. | Wald | df | Sig. |
| --- | --- | --- | --- | --- | --- |
| Overcrowd | .129 | .071 | 3.300 | 1 | .069 |
| PCE | 1.084 | 1.164 | .867 | 1 | .352 |
| TSL | -1.294 | 1.887 | .470 | 1 | .493 |
| PIOC | .070 | .132 | .285 | 1 | .594 |
| Lib | -1.123 | 1.146 | .960 | 1 | .327 |
| Midwest | -3.910 | 3.105 | 1.586 | 1 | .208 |
| South | 3.162 | 3.029 | 1.090 | 1 | .297 |
| West | -3.120 | 3.316 | .885 | 1 | .347 |
| Prof | .244 | .217 | 1.259 | 1 | .262 |
| Year | .915 | .471 | 3.771 | 1 | .052 |
| Court | .067 | .188 | .126 | 1 | .723 |
| Prisoners | .079 | .057 | 1.897 | 1 | .168 |
| Constant | -26.388 | 13.210 | 3.991 | 1 | .046 |

Dependent variable: The magnitude of SPP in 2003.

# APPENDIX I. GLM RESULTS OF SPP DATA

Generalized linear models                  No. of obs = 50
Optimization: ML: Newton-Raphson           Residual df = 37
                                           Scale parameter = 1
Deviance = 168.9575099                     (1/df)       Deviance      =
4.566419
Pearson = 3.011907491                      (1/df) Pearson = .0814029

Variance function: V(u) = u*(1-u)          [Bernoulli]
Link function: g(u) = ln(u/(1-u))          [Logit]
Standard errors: Sandwich

Log pseudo-likelihood = -7.669288086 AIC = .8267715
BIC = 24.21265868

|            | Coef.   | Std Err | p-value |
|------------|---------|---------|---------|
| Overcrowd  | 0.035   | 0.013   | 0.006   |
| PCE        | -0.031  | 0.165   | 0.853   |
| TSL        | 0.2238  | 0.348   | 0.522   |
| PIOC       | 0.014   | 0.046   | 0.759   |
| Lib        | -0.518  | 0.276   | 0.060   |
| Midwest    | -0.716  | 1.107   | 0.518   |
| South      | 1.058   | 0.822   | 0.198   |
| West       | 1.388   | 0.817   | 0.090   |
| Prof       | 0.054   | 0.043   | 0.203   |
| Year       | 0.154   | 0.040   | 0.000   |
| Court      | -0.023  | 0.020   | 0.240   |
| Prisoners  | -0.007  | 0.006   | 0.229   |
| Cons       | -9.695  | 1.799   | 0.000   |

Dependent variable: The magnitude of SPP in 2003.

# APPENDIX J. OLS RESULTS OF SPP DATA

a. Model summary

| Model | R | R-square | Adjusted R-square |
|-------|---|----------|-------------------|
|       | 0.732 | 0.536 | 0.39 |

b. NOVA results

| Model | Sum of Squares | df | Mean Square | F | sig |
|-------|----------------|----|-------------|---|-----|
| Regression | 2882.6 | 12 | 240.2 | 3.567 | 0.001 |
| Residual | 2491.9 | 37 | 67.3 | | |
| Total | 5374.5 | 49 | | | |

c. OLS coefficients

| | Unstandardized Coefficients | | Standardized Coefficients | t | sig |
|--|------|-----------|------|------|------|
| | B | Std Error | Beta | | |
| Constant | -25.747 | 15.189 | | -1.695 | .098 |
| Overcrowd | .155 | .093 | .234 | 1.673 | .103 |
| PCE | -.385 | 1.324 | -.048 | -.291 | .773 |
| TSL | 2.793 | 2.808 | .135 | .995 | .326 |
| PIOC | .229 | .290 | .159 | .789 | .435 |
| Lib | -2.234 | 2.020 | -.206 | -1.106 | .276 |
| Midwest | -2.114 | 4.193 | -.087 | -.504 | .617 |
| South | 5.365 | 5.536 | .241 | .969 | .339 |
| West | 7.715 | 4.437 | .326 | 1.739 | .090 |
| Prof | .286 | .294 | .119 | .972 | .337 |
| Year | .910 | .307 | .453 | 2.968 | .005 |
| Court | -.201 | .155 | -.190 | -1.302 | .201 |
| Prisoners | -.056 | .054 | -.179 | -1.032 | .309 |

Dependent variable: The magnitude of SPP in 2003.

# INDEX

**D**

**E**